See my

ISBN **978-0-9891187-0-5**

Dedicated to our loved ones who continually love and support us.

Other Books by Baylor Barbee & Trent Shelton

Breaking Your Own Heart

Upcoming Books by Baylor Barbee & Trent Shelton

The Games We Play

Life after Sports

Championship Mindset

Still Breaking Your Own Heart

101 Things I'd Teach a Younger Me

Minor Setback, Major Comeback

Table of Contents

Introduction

Find a person complacent with their past and problems and there you'll find the mindset of most people. Find a person determined to overcome those problems and there you'll see a leader.

We've all made mistakes and we all have problems. All of us have made mistakes we'd like to forget and most of us may not be content with where we are, but we do wish to see a better tomorrow. If you picked up this book it's because you, despite your situation, strive to progress in life; you are choosing to rise above what you used to be to become a better person and create a better future.

We're by no means saying that you have to have any deep dark scandalous past to benefit from this book. If you're honest with yourself, there is always some part of your past that you either regret, or there are actions you took or didn't take that have prevented you from being where you want to be thus far. Together, we're going to embark on a figurative, thirty-day journey designed to help you free yourself from who you were and become that person you want to be.

If you're wondering what page the "secret formula" is on to fix your problems, we can settle that right here.

Are you ready for the secret? Here it is. *All Change starts with you.* Repeat it to yourself. "Change starts with you." People can pray for you, encourage you, or hope for your future, but until you decide you want it for yourself, nothing else matters. If you've picked up this book to escape a past and create a better future, we commend you. It takes a big person to admit things aren't going exactly how they'd like and an even bigger person to do something about it.

Deep down, you know how to fix your problems. Let us rephrase that. The answers to your problems are inside you, you alone can fix them. Our goal here is not to be dictators who force you to follow some crazy exact steps or else face failure. We're not here to tell you this is the only way to progress. We are telling you this is an effective, tried and true method that works.

Picture this book, more or less, as a tour guide for your journey, not your boss. Each situation is different, and every person has unique problems and a unique past as well as different goals or destinations they are trying to reach. Some of you will move faster than others - we're not concerned with getting to the finish line first; we're concerned with you getting to your future as a solid, positive individual living the life you desire.

We encourage you to break the book down into a chapter a day and really focus on that chapter. If it takes more than a day to grasp a concept, by all means, take your time. A solid house cannot be built without a firm foundation. Each step builds on top of each other; so if you don't grasp one, go back. It's a lot better to take it slow and get your desired results than to get to the finish line of the journey and have learned nothing.

Our aim is not to give you the how-to's of self-help. If you're looking for that, please put this book down and grab a title by an author with decades of experience into the scientific psychology of the mind. We are here to help provoke thoughts in your head and awaken parts of your mind and soul that will help you come to conclusions.

We're not trying to bog you down with complex terminology and scientific discoveries in human potential, but rather putting an effective formula for change into a frame of reference you can relate to. We're not trying to paint the picture of your future for you, we're only trying to give you the guidance and tools necessary to create the future you want, despite the past or problems you have had.

Like we said, you have the answers - we're here to help you get them out. When you succeed in leaving your past and creating a great future for yourself, you'll have yourself to thank.

Remember, this is a journey. Not everyone gets to a destination in the same amount of time. It is a 30-day journey, but take as long as you need to get there. We're after genuine change from who you were to who you will be, not world records for reaching your destination.

Change starts with you. Change Starts now

Skeletons in Your Closet

Day 1 – Admit You have a Problem

In hearing his unmistakable voice raise as the instrumentation picks up, all of us at some point, have sang along with Michael Jackson… "That's why I want you to know – I'm starting with the Man in the Mirror. I'm asking him to make a change."

Truer words were never spoken, yet fewer words were ever harder to put into action. They say a journey of a thousand miles starts with a single step. In an effort to free yourself from your past over the next thirty days, which may seem like a 1000 miles to you, you have to start with the first step. Like any worthwhile accomplishment, this one is the most difficult.

The reality is that we live in a world filled with finger pointing, casting blame, and deciding fault. Whether it's political groups battling over who ruined the economy, businessmen blaming others for stock prices plummeting, or couples arguing over why their relationship is not working, the status quo says this, "Admit no wrong, yet find and point out the faults in others."

Guess what? You're not reading this book because you want to be part of the status quo, aka average. You're reading this book because you want to rise above it. They say if you do the opposite of what everyone else is doing, you will most likely be successful. That's exactly what you have to do. While everyone else is pointing fingers at other, step number one is to point the finger at the man in the mirror. Regardless of your past, or where you're at, *the man (or woman) in the mirror is entirely at fault for everything.*

Your impulse after reading that last paragraph was probably to think of a million excuses and events that weren't your "fault" that caused you to be in the situation you're in. One of the biggest misconceptions in life is that we're supposed to be error free, or that we're not supposed to admit we have problems. We take the dirt in our lives; throw it at others, without realizing we're only digging ourselves into a bigger hole.

Admitting you have a problem is difficult - we never said the journey would be easy. If it were easy, everyone would do it! So many of us spend our lives trying to hide our skeletons in the closet and put on a mask for the world. We continue to head in a downward spiral by telling ourselves we have no control of the situation.

Have you ever been around someone who you know for a fact doesn't shower; they just spray on a bunch of cologne or perfume to try and mask the smell? Despite the outwardly pleasant smell, the inner wretched smell permeates through the air. We all hate being around those people, right? Skeletons in a closet are no different. You can hide them, mask them, use them as Halloween decorations, but they're still skeletons. They're still there and they still stink. In your life, you're the janitor, the only one that can acknowledge where the problem is, and the only one in charge of cleaning it up.

Have you ever found yourself driving the wrong way down a freeway? While going Seventy miles per hour do you immediately jerk the wheel, spin one hundred and eighty degrees and floor it the other way? Probably not - and why? Because your car would flip, you'd wreck and could hurt yourself or worse. Many people try to fix the problems in their lives in that manner though. In an effort to make sure people don't see their mistakes, they try and instantly turn things around, yet the negative momentum they've built up causes them to crash.

In order to go the right way in life, we must first admit that we're going the wrong way. In doing this, we only need to recognize that we're going the wrong way, pullover and STOP. We don't have to make a daredevil high-speed turn. We just need to come to a complete stop before we go any further down the wrong path. Only when we come to a stop are we able to analyze where we're truly at.

The ultimate goal of what we're trying to accomplish is a positive transformation, and that begins with a positive mindset. Regardless of what you're trying to overcome, take a minute and look at your current state of affairs and take responsibility for them. In doing this you have taken the most important step. Taking ownership of your faults gives you power, not weakness. Would you rather be a passenger in a boat heading towards becoming a shipwreck and hopelessly hope someone else saves the day, or would you rather be the captain and have the opportunity to save your life?

Now utter these four simple words:

"It is MY Fault."

Good, now look yourself in the mirror, let out a deep breath and say this:

"I have a problem."

Congratulations, you have just freed yourself from being a passenger on the "life pushes and blows me where it wants to" ship that's headed for imminent danger. Instead, you have become the captain of your own life, your own dreams, and a brighter future.

Think of your brain as a CEO of a company, solely in charge of making sure everything is going correctly in its company (your body). When you have a physical injury, the brain sends information to the body that says "Hey we have a problem here, let's work together and fix this," and your body goes to work healing itself. By consciously admitting you have a problem, your brain is going to do the same thing. It is going to be more keenly aware of situations regarding that problem as well as do everything in its power to fix the problem. So, by simply admitting you have a problem, you have turned yourself from an enemy to an ally.

By uttering those four simple words, "I have a problem," you have aligned your heart and mind to work together to rectify that past. Now that we have "team YOU" formed, let's go tackle our first opponent…Pride.

Quick Points

- The first step in a process is often most difficult
- The status quo is to point the finger at others
- In order to turn your life around, you must first stop going the wrong direction – come to a complete stop.
- Say this, "I have a problem."

Ponder This

Do I want to continue to let my past dictate my future or will I admit I have a problem so that I can begin fixing it?

Who's at fault for everything? Why is this a good thing?

Why does masking a problem make the situation worse?

What should I do when I realize I'm headed the wrong way?

Day 2 – Humble Yourself

It is human nature to want to side with the stronger side in any situation. If you were a sports star you'd want to play for the championship team rather than the last place team. You'd rather be the CEO of a fortune 500 company than a struggling company that is about to fold. However, we often go against the bibles instructions to humble ourselves, in lieu of pride. 1 Peter 5:5 says "God opposes the haughty ones." Translation, God, also known as "the best team" is against prideful people.

In an effort to rid ourselves of our past and move forward, we need all the help we can get. If that's not enough for you, let's take a deeper look at pride. Pride, or lack of humility, is 99.9% a mental steroid that increases the effect of almost every problem. Pride is the barrier between failure and success. It's the lying voice in your head that says, "You're fine on this path, and you don't need to turn around." If you can't find a problem in your life or a fault, Pride has you fooled and you're losing a great fight.

Pride likes to play an eternal game of hide and seek with us. It's extremely sneaky and not only hides from us, but when we search for it, it convinces us that we need to hide as well. Pride will enable us to hide our problems, our faults, and not let anyone find out we're imperfect; therefore, passing the blame on others. It's highly convincing in its argument.

We all have pride, some of us more than others, but in Day 2 of this journey, we need to humble ourselves. To do so, we must be able to identify our prideful ways and more importantly be able to let it go. Pride will be trying to rear its ugly head back into our journey as we get closer toward succeeding in our transformation. Remember pride is the warrior that your past uses to try and keep you from evolving into a better person.

Now that may sound silly to you; thinking of pride as a warrior trying to keep you from moving forward. However, for just a second, truly personify pride. Think of pride as the Goliath in your life trying to defeat you, think of pride as that friend who's always giving you bad advice, or feel pride as that itch on your skin that bothers you all day. In doing this you will start picking up on aspects of your life that pride affects. It's okay if it becomes more noticeable. It's better to see pride in everything that you do rather than to continue thinking you have no pride.

Do you know how gold, silver, iron and other metals are purified? They are put through the fire, in which they lose common metals and other elements. Though they may seem weaker in the refining and purification process, they end up pure and strong. There's a misconception that humbling yourself means admitting weakness, which ultimately makes you weaker. Think of pride as the common metals in your sword of life. The more of it you remove in this stage, the stronger your sword is going to be when the real battle starts later in this journey.

You wouldn't knowingly put yourself in an adverse position before any competitive event, so don't start the journey with a sword full of pride.

Still some of us think we can move forward without letting go of our pride. Just remember, pride plays for the other team. You may think you can carry it, but all along your journey pride is telling the enemy what you're doing and receiving information from the enemy to give you deceptive and self-sabotaging advice. *Pride is the hungry lion telling the gazelle it should veer off from the pack and walk down this grassy knoll alone.*

Aside from that, pride is heavy. If you wanted to win a race and the option of running by yourself or running with a 100-pound bag of sand strapped to your back, what would you choose? No brainer right? Why is it then, in an effort to let go of our pasts and move into our future do we choose to let pride weigh us down? Pride is that 100-pound weight that we carry around for no reason. Not only does it slow us down, it's burdensome, and often makes us burn out and quit before we reach a finish line or goal we could have reached a long time ago.

We over-illustrate the importance of letting go of pride for the simple fact that pride is the Achilles heel in which our past will use to try and sneak up and catch up with us again as we continue to fortify our minds and focus on our futures. Most of the success or failures of the great challenges we'll face in the next few weeks will be solely based on our ability to relinquish pride and humble ourselves.

When you truly let go of pride, you are not only showing yourself that you're serious about change, you're showing God and you're showing those around you. *Letting go of pride is an action*, and we all know actions speak louder than words. Pride wants to hold onto you because it needs you to survive, you don't need it.

In the medical world you know what we call that? Cancer. Do yourself a favor and get rid of the cancer called pride and continue on your journey.

"Whoever honors himself will be humbled, and whoever humbles himself will be honored." Matthew 23:12. You have two options. *Humble yourself now so that the world can eventually see your greatness or show yourself greatness now and eventually the world will expose you and show your flaws.*

Quick Points

- God opposes prideful people
- Pride is the steroid that increases every problem
- We must admit we have pride then release it
- Pride is a cancer that needs you; you don't need it.

Ponder This

In what ways do I most struggle with pride?

What does foolish pride do?

Why do I hold onto pride when I know it weighs me down?

Day 3 – Define the Problem

How many times have you started getting sick and ignored it, telling yourself it's not a big deal? How many times have you heard your vehicle making a funny noise but chose to ignore it? What happens in both situations? It gets WORSE. We often see athletes play on what they believed to be was just a bruised bone or muscle. We all know what happens next; they tear a muscle or shatter a bone, turning a problem that could have been fixed quickly into a season ending or career ending injury.

Why do we let problems continue to coexist with us when we know they're there? Most often it's fear. We're afraid that if we find out what the problem is, that it might be worse than we think. We're afraid if we go get that cold checked out, that it could be a disease. We're afraid that if we get that squeaky noise in a car checked out, that the mechanic would tell us it's a problem that will cost a lot of money to fix. Because of fear, we go on ignoring that elephant in the room, (pronounced problem), and hope it goes away. Ask yourself this, has any big problem in your life ever gone away without you addressing it?

Before we can define our problem in day 3 we have to address fear. If we try and define the problem with fear in our hearts, we may cheat ourselves and admit a watered down problem that is far easier to fix than the true problem.

"God has not given us a spirit of fear, but of power, love, and a sound mind." 2 Timothy 1:7. If God gives us power, love and a sound mind, then where do you think Fear comes from? *Fear is nothing but faith in the Devil.* Fear, along with pride, is the Devil's main weapon in an attempt to tie you to the past you're trying to escape and to keep you from reaching your bright future.

Once we realize fear is nothing but a mind trick we play on ourselves, we can set it aside and continue on with our journey.... next stop? Define Problem Avenue.

This is a tough street. It is the road less traveled, because the scenery isn't pretty. Guess what? The Caves and rocks in the mountains of Sierra Leone aren't pretty either but there are diamonds hidden there. The flat dusty lands of West Texas are the opposite of gorgeous, but the land contains billions of dollars' worth of oil.

How do you get those diamonds and that oil? You have to figure out what obstacles you will face and how to get through the rocks and land formations to get to the treasure. In a sense, you have to define the problem. *Trying to fix a problem without defining it is like heading toward a destination without any sense of direction.*

If a friend you'd never visited called you and said, "Come visit" without giving an address or directions, it'd be almost impossible to get there. We know it exists, but we can't get there without a frame of reference. The same goes for working toward a brighter future and overcoming a past. We can acknowledge that a problem is there but if we don't define the problem, we can never fix it.

It takes a strong person to complete this step, and this is not a step that you should take lightly. If you don't accurately define your problem, then you will likely spend the next 27 days fixing the wrong aspect of yourself.

What would happen if you had an aching headache, but somehow the doctor diagnosed your problem as an upset stomach? He would likely give you medication to ease your stomach and follow all the steps necessary to make your stomach feel better. What's the problem here? Yep, he's fixing a problem that you didn't have. Yes we're sure it's an effective solution to a problem, but not to your problem.

The same goes with misdiagnosing or incorrectly defining our problem. If we define the problem at hand incorrectly we won't get better. If we don't fully define our problem, we won't be able to fix all of it. Problems are a lot like weeds, if you don't kill all of them, they come back stronger than before.

There's an upside to defining the problem. It gives you a clear precise target to overcome. It helps you remove fear because you now know what you have to defeat.

If your life depended on a fight between you and an opponent and you had a month to train, would you rather know who your opponent was and be able to study everything about them, or would you just want to show up on fight day and see your opponent for the first time? By defining the problem, we now have a clear vision of where we're headed and what we're facing.

When we know the problem with the car, the diagnosis of the sickness, or the address of the friend's house, we can work toward the desired result. Knowing our problem puts us one step closer to fixing it.

At times during this journey you'll feel alone. Take a moment right now to briefly congratulate yourself on having taken three very important steps.

Also, while you're doing that, be sure and listen to yourself. Much like when you feel you're lost when traveling, a small voice tells you something's not right, you're lost, or you're going the wrong way, you may have not completed one of the past few days to the best of your ability. Or you may have realized something you didn't before such as some pride you still had that you thought you rid yourself of.

Don't feel like you have to "learn on the run," it's perfectly okay to go back a day or two and really grasp the concepts. We are here to make solid changes in our lives and move toward a better future. It's better to arrive at the end of the journey in forty days knowing you've given your all and made permanent changes, than to sprint to the end and have learned nothing.
Remember the methodical tortoise always beats the rabbit.

If you were building a house, would you rather the contractor take too much time to ensure perfect calculations on the foundation of the house or just sprint through it to "get it done."?

These are foundational days, so it's important that you set a solid foundation on which to continue this journey in a manner most conducive to success.

Quick Points

- We often let problems stay with us out of fear of how bad they could be.
- Fear is faith in the devil
- It takes courage to accurately define a problem
- Defining a problem gives you a clear vision of what you need to overcome

Ponder This

What has fear kept you from doing?

What happens when you ignore problems in your life?

Now define your problem. Write it Down!

Day 4 – Why do you have the Problem

It's been a rough past three days and you may be feeling like you're doing nothing but surrounding yourself with negative thoughts and vibes. While that may be true in a sense, it's all based on the perspective in which you view it. If you've viewed the past few days as a waste of time, wondering when were "getting to the good stuff" then you've missed the point. If you've carefully followed these steps and applied them to your life, then you don't view it as surrounding yourself with the past you're trying to move on from, but rather you are setting yourself up for success by figuring out where you have failed before so that you do not repeat it. If you're one of those people, let's continue.

If you've really bought into freeing yourself from your past and moving on, you may have gone what some would consider overboard. By that, we're saying you may have a huge list of problems that you have identified and are wondering how you can possibly fix in 30 days. It's great that you have identified all those problems, because it's better to do too much than too little, today is going to help take some of the load off.

We used a vehicle problem example yesterday and a sickness example as well. Today, we're going to continue by drilling down further into the problem. We're going to figure out why we have the problem that we do. By doing this you'll start to realize that a lot of the "millions of problems" you think you have in life often stem from one source, one problem. Taking care of the deep root problem will clear up the surface level "issues."

Sometimes we define our car as "something wrong with the engine" or define a sickness as "something wrong with our head," but we have to take a deeper look at it to figure out the cause of the problem. A mechanic may look at an engine and find that it's making a noise because a certain part is out of line, which causes not only the car to squeak, but other parts to break down as well. A doctor may find that you have swelling in your brain which causing extra pressure on your head, giving you the headache. But why are the parts out of line and why is there swelling? That's what doctors and mechanics figure out.

Similarly, when we look deeper into our stack of problems to figure out why we do it, we usually find the true problem. We think we'd all agree from the outside that an alcoholic's problem is alcohol. But if you gave an alcoholic a truth serum and asked them why they drink, very few, if any would say it's solely because they just like to drink. Most would tell you they drink to avoid reality, to cover up their sorrows, hide the pain, etc. They drink because they're unhappy not because they like alcohol. By uncovering why they drink (unhappiness), we have revealed the true issue that we need to fix. It's not the alcohol that's the problem, it's the empty unhappy feeling. If we fix that, more than likely we'll cure the "issue" which is the alcohol.

If we looked at a serial cheater, we would probably say the problem is cheating. We're not saying that's not "a" problem, we're saying it's not really "the" problem. The truth is most serial cheaters cheat out of insecurity. They need to know that they're wanted; they need to know that they're desirable to others.

They cheat to temporarily fill that void. That's "why" they do it. Alcoholics drink to escape reality of their perceived situations, and that's "why" they do it.

Are you starting to see things in a different light? You should be. By no means is it our goal to downplay alcoholism, cheating, or any other "past problem." What we are trying to do is help you realize that whatever it is you struggle with, is probably not because of why everyone else tells you it is. We're not handing out victim cards here or pity parties, but it's important for you to understand why you do what you do so you can get a better grip on fixing the situation.

Reevaluate the problems you wrote down before. Are they problems or are they issues of the problem? Is there an underlying problem? Do you see how by fixing that problem you will fix the issues associated with it? Isn't it comforting knowing you don't have as many problems to fix as you thought?

This may have opened you up to a new level of awareness about the journey you're on or the past you're battling. If that's so, remember its ok to go back and check out day 3 and redefine your problem.

1 Corinthians 9:24 and the passages surrounding it speak of running a race in such a way as to get the eternal prize. What its saying is, run a solid pure race, attack this journey in solid steps, even if it means taking a step back to be sure you're doing it correctly. Just because someone gets to the finish line first doesn't mean they won. Just ask the hundreds of Olympic athletes who have cheated, won, and later had their medals taken away and given to the righteous competitor, and were shamed publicly on a world stage.

Quick Points

- It's better to have acknowledged too many problems than to few
- Most "problems" we think we have are merely issues of a larger problem
- If you uncover the root problem, it will be easier to correct your issues.

Ponder This

What is the difference between an issue and a problem?

What are my issues?

What is my problem?

Day 5 – How is the problem affecting your life?

Thousands of years ago Lao Tzu said it best when he said, "To know thyself, know thy enemy and a thousand battles, a thousand victories." The point he is making is that in addition to knowing ourselves, we must know the enemy of our situation, which is currently our problem. Today we're going to analyze this problem and how it is affecting us. Upon realizing how it's truly affecting us, we are creating a strong motivation to change it. This will be beneficial down the road when the journey gets difficult and we want to turn back.

Insurance salesmen often make fortunes off residuals. A residual is something that continues to happen after the main event of the situation. Insurance salesman strike a deal with a new client, and make residual profit for years to come off of that initial deal. This is great for positive situations like income; however, we have to be aware that problems, like our pasts, have residual effects.

Many of us tie our past or overall problems to one or maybe a couple of extremely big events. While that may have been a big factor in your past, often times it's the residual that truly does the damage.

Let's take the alcoholic from the other day. On a "here and now" level the alcohol is affecting his liver, but what's the residual? The hangover from the alcohol causes him to want to sleep a little longer. Because of that, he misses work more often, and ultimately losing his job. Without a job, his family life is affected. It's all residual effects of the big problem.

In the olden days (and still to this day), people had a "problem" with faith. They refused to believe what they could not see. For eighty to one hundred years people on the earth laughed as Noah built this large ark. Noah informed them of the flood to come; day-by-day he built the boat, day-by-day people on the earth didn't believe him. If you're familiar with the bible then you know how that story ended for those who didn't realize how the problem of not having faith affected their situation. A great flood filled the earth, not only affecting their lives, but also taking their lives. In a sense our problems do the same thing. They may start out as a light drizzle, however overtime the rains get stronger and floods come. We have made no "ark" to save ourselves because we don't see how the downpour of problems could affect us until we drown in them.

Every decade or so there is a large oil spill in our oceans. We all see on the television the immediate effects on the land, the birds, polar bears, and fish all being covered in oil and washed up on the shore. Weeks later we see heartfelt commercials by the oil companies telling their story and what they're doing to "clean up" the spill. What they don't tell you are the residual effects that "problem" has on the environment. They don't tell you about how the marine life has been affected so much that the next few years of seafood in that region will be scarce due to the killing off of the marine life that populate the area. The problem doesn't just stop when you fix the main issue; the residuals continue to cause harm.

If you're blind to how it's affecting your life, you won't see your problem as a "problem." Unfortunately, I think we all know someone in our lives that were a little sick and did nothing about it. They got increasingly tired, but blamed fatigue on other things such as work or school. Finally the problem got so bad that once they did get checked out and found out that something was seriously wrong, like a tumor, it caused the residual problem to multiply all over the body.

These may seem like gruesome illustrations, however, the point is that if we don't see how the problem is truly affecting our lives, we won't be able to truly change it. Just like yesterday, if we don't understand the entire scope of the problem, it will catch back up with us.

Problems are silent assassins. They don't kill you overnight, but day after day they slowly kill your hopes and dreams, your good attitude, your relationship with God, and your ability to move into a great future.

Quick Points

- To defeat our problem, we have to know it
- Residuals are continued benefits or hindrances of an initial event
- If you're blind to how a problem is affecting your life, it will consume you
- Problems are silent assassins, slowly killing you

Ponder This

How are my problems affecting my quality of life?

What areas of my life are my problems having residual negative effects on?

Am I fixing problems or putting Band-Aids on issues?

Day 6 – Who else has the problem affected?

There comes a point in every real relationship where "it gets serious." In the journey we're on with ourselves, today is that day. Up until this point we have focused inwardly on ourselves and tried to discover the root of our past and clearly define all aspects of our main problem. If you're reading this book to escape a past and move to a future, there's a good chance you're not just doing it for you, you're probably doing it for those you care about as well. As with problems, we often downplay the effect it has on others rather than to face the reality of the situation.

There are several stages along this journey that we consider "meltdown stages." That means that if you're really into this journey, completing these stages are extremely difficult. If you have a meltdown during today's exercise, don't view it as a bad thing. Don't view yourself as a bad person. Rather, realize the breakdown is just a testament to how much you care. This will give you added motivation to continue to improve yourself so that you never cry these same tears or force others to cry them.

It might cause a meltdown because up until this point we have been slowly opening our eyes to the truth, and today we're going to get blinded by it.

We've always said that if you live life for yourself, you can't be truly happy. When you live life for someone else, there you will find true happiness. The same can be said for problems. As people we shouldn't like hurting ourselves, more importantly, we definitely shouldn't want to hurt others. It's time to take a big look at whom all we've affected with our past. Open your eyes, because it's probably more people than you think.

There will be an impulse to downplay the effects of the problem on certain people. We may write people off in manners like "oh well he/she deserved it," or, "we're not that close anyways." If that's you then we encourage you to re-read day 1 and 2 and remember, "It's YOUR fault" and not to let the pride get the best of you here. Pride will make a solid attempt today to thwart your journey.

The first thing you have to realize is that problems are unfaithful. They're not committed to you; and they will never rest alone. They will always find another bed to rest in. Therefore your problems that you think are only yours, are doing their best to invade the lives and spirits of those around you.

Think back a few days ago when we looked at the foundation of the problem and saw how far it reached. Now look at that same foundation and everyone in your life that walks on it. Write down the Friends, Family, Co-Workers, etc. that your problem has affected. Look at your problem as an oil spill, and find out who all has been soaked in oil. All people are affected, but make a special note of those most deeply affected by your situation. Similarly to an earthquake, those closest to the area where the eruption happened are more devastated and affected by the disaster than those further out.

If you're telling yourself that your problem is ONLY affecting you, then please put a bookmark on this page and go back to day 2. Pride is blinding you. Remember, this journey is not a race to get their first. No one will give you a medal for getting their first, because your prize comes from getting there correctly.

Whether your problem stems from a drug habit, or you're habitually poor with time management, it affects others. The money you spend on drugs or the time you lose in hangovers and recovery is both time and money lost out on those that could have benefited from it. When you're continually late, you disrespect people by not valuing their time, you are throwing their schedules out of alignment.

It takes a big person to admit when they're wrong, and it takes an even bigger person to admit that they've wronged others. We're not quite ready to face those we've affected yet, but we do need to realize who all has been affected.

It's also important to realize at this point, that you may not be, and probably aren't, affecting those around you purposely. In fact, your intention may have been the exact opposite. We see star athletes who play through injuries to try and help their team. However, that ankle injury problem causes them to not be able to give 100% and therefore become a hindrance to their team.

You may not be a professional athlete, but in your own unique way, though you may have had good intentions. However, your problem can affect others.

You may have promised your family you'd be home for dinner at six. Yet due to your poor time management skills, you stay at the office until eight. Your underlying motive may have been to make money to provide for your family, but the residual of your problem puts distrust and disappointment into the minds of your family members.

Usually problems aren't isolated incidents; therefore, continuing that trend, you become undependable to those around you. You continue to live with a smile because you feel you're doing it for them and they understand it. Yet all they are doing is building feelings of animosity and bitterness.

That can spiral to a point to where your family and friends want nothing to do with you. Now on top of poor time management, you must deal with the repercussions of a shattered family life.

The devil used to be an elite angel in heaven. He struggled with jealously and disobedience. On top of him getting kicked out of heaven, we now have to suffer and deal with him on earth.

That's why it's a meltdown stage, few of us truly want to hurt others, and it's a sobering thought to realize not only the number of people we've affected, but also more importantly trying to get a grasp on how deeply we've affected them.

If you're truly in tune with this journey, today probably stings more than any of the previous days. Realize that is part of the healing process. If you're hurting, that is the compassion in you wanting to rectify your situation. Consider that a positive, and consider that growth. Sometimes, what feels like a step back, is really a step forward.

Often times, people can walk fine before an ACL surgery, and after the surgery, are on crutches for months. It seemed like a step back, but dealing with the pain of the surgery was strengthening them for the long run.

Our journey is a long one, dealing with the pain of realizing who we've hurt is not pleasant, but it's an extremely pivotal and necessary landmark to cross on our road to a brighter future.

Quick Points

- If you live for yourself you can't be truly happy. Living for others is the basis of happiness.
- Your problems always affect more than just you
- It takes a strong person to admit when they're wrong, it takes a bigger one to admit when they've wrong others.
- Problems are unfaithful. They not only want to affect you, they want to affect those around you
- If you had a meltdown in realizing who you've hurt, consider it progress not a setback

Ponder This

Who has my problem affected and how deeply can I see that it has affected them?

In what ways did my problem grow to be this big?

Day 7 – What causes the problem?

Have you ever had a family pet that was harmless, and one day, it just snaps and goes crazy? What caused that?

The answer lies in this question. What is it that causes a bullet to fire out of the barrel of a rifle? The Answer: the Trigger.

We all have triggers that can push us over the edge. Often times you hear people's excuse for acting in a manner that they normally wouldn't by saying "they pushed my buttons." We're all familiar with that. If you have a spouse, a child, or someone close to you then more than likely they know how to push your buttons. We all have them.

The problem is not that we have buttons, it's that we don't think about those buttons other than to say they've been pushed. Today our goal is to label those buttons.

Imagine you were sitting in the cockpit of a plane with no parachute staring at two sets of buttons. You know that one sequence initiated an autopilot program that would get you safely to your destination, while the other was an ejection sequence that would launch you into the sky miles into the air. Knowing that one sequence could be detrimental to your life wouldn't you hope that the maker of the plane properly labeled the buttons so that you would know what was happening as you completed the sequence of knobs and buttons? On top of that, if it was the ejection sequence, wouldn't you want a voice activated control to *Warn* you of what you were doing and what was about to happen if you pressed the final button?

We would hope so. Why is it then, we don't place the same labels on the triggers in our lives that set off our problems. We're the maker of the plane, so it's our job to make sure that we can readily identify the steps toward our "ejection" or blast off, and to make others aware of it.

We often give children the benefit of the doubt when they mess up because "they didn't know better." They didn't know the rules, therefore they didn't know their actions would produce the result it did. However, when someone pulls one of our triggers, we snap on them. Why? Did they know our triggers? Did we label our buttons?

Probably not. And it doesn't have to be people. A lot of times we're pressing the sequence of our own buttons and initiate our problem. What if we actually observed our own buttons, and see what caused us to do the things we do. Let's do that.

There is usually a certain sequence of events that leads us all to dive into our problem. Let's look at our alcoholic friend from the last chapter.

The alcoholic doesn't just say, "I need a drink" and gets one. There was a sequence. There is something that triggered his need. He may be having a good day, and all of a sudden he's alone and feels "lonely." (THE TRIGGER.) He then starts to tell himself he doesn't have any friends and no one cares about him (he's just hit number one). He may then tell himself he wants to forget about the loneliness (number two), and finally turns to alcohol to solve his problem...BLASTOFF (button number three).

You see there were numerous signs, numerous buttons that were pressed to get to the problem. If he were to label those triggers, he would be able to change the outcome of the situation. Instead of ejecting himself, he could have had a smoother ride.

By recognizing our triggers, we are able to realize the path we're on and change it. Let's say our alcoholic friend recognized what triggered him, how might his steps be different?

He feels lonely (SAME TRIGGER). However now instead of jumping right to his former step two, he may hit a new button instead. He may hit the "I do have friends and family that cares about me, let me reach out to them.) If they're not available he may go do something that will benefit them, like shop for a gift for his spouse or kids. The result of that can be nothing but positive, and there are many paths he could take, but it all started with the trigger.

There is always a trigger to a problem. A light can't turn on without someone flipping the switch, a car can't start without turning on the ignition, and a problem can't start unless it's triggered. A bullet can't fire without the trigger being pulled, and participation in a problem can't start unless a trigger initiates it.

Think about your own main problem. If you look hard enough, you'll realize there are events, at least one, usually a few that push us into our problems. Think about everyone that "pushes your buttons," or "drives you to drink." Now take your focus off the person and put it on the action in which pushes you toward relapsing into your problem.

Take a few minutes out of your day to get out your imaginary sharpie and label the triggers and buttons in mind that set off a sequence of self-destruction. Labeling these triggers will help you to realize them when they arise so that you have a better chance of channeling your energies in a positive manner that will help your future than a repeated action that will keep you in your past.

Quick Points

- Triggers initiate problems
- There is usually a sequence of events that push us back into repeating our problems
- Put labels on the triggers and buttons in your life

Ponder This

What are the triggers in your life?

What is the button sequence to initiate your triggers?

Day 8 – Risk / Reward

Are you a lofty dreamer? Do you often fantasize about all the great things life could bring you? Or are you the opposite? Do you spend your days thinking about the negative repercussions if a certain event happens or if something doesn't get done?

Is there a right or wrong way? Absolutely not. Different things work for different people. It is important though to figure out if your mind is one that goes towards pleasure or avoids pain. By first figuring out if you're a pleasure seeker or pain avoider, you'll understand how you need to talk to yourself in order to be most effective, as we get further into today.

For example, if you're someone who always sees the glass half full, when thinking about your problem that you're trying to overcome, it's not going to be beneficial for you to list a bunch of negative things that will happen if you don't fix the problem. On the other hand, if you write a list of all the glorious things that could transpire if you fix the problem, your mind will perk up…. you're speaking your own language.

If you're more of a pain avoider, then telling yourself how great it will be to fix your problem is not going to resonate as well with yourself as if you make a list of all the bad things that could happen if you don't fix the problem.

Again, there is nothing wrong with either one. Just take a few minutes and think about yourself and figure out which you are. By speaking to yourself in a manner that is more impactful, you have a better chance of getting to where you want to be. We call it "firing on all cylinders."

Let's now examine the risks versus rewards of solving our problem. If you're a glass half full type then you're going to want to pay special attention to the rewards of succeeding in fixing a problem. If you're more of a pessimistic type, pay attention to the risks of not fixing your problem. These will serve as motivators you can keep in your back pocket when the journey gets tough and you need motivation to continue.

To make your list of *Risks,* ask yourself this:

If I continue to do what I'm doing, what will happen?

To make a list of rewards ask yourself this:

If I stop this now, how will it benefit my life?

Pretend you're Marty McFly for a second here and look into the future. Give yourself an honest assessment of the results of both questions.

Problems have an appetite as well. You either feed your problem, or you starve it until it no longer exists. By using the *risk vs. rewards* based on your pleasure/pain personality, you can use those thoughts to help feed your future and starve your past instead of the other way around.

Nothing in life is stagnant. Think of life as an uphill journey. If you put your car in neutral, you may think you're standing still, but you are rolling backwards down the hill. The same goes for problems. You are either correcting them or making them worse. They are never just sitting there.

Now take this time to really write out the pros and cons of correcting your problem to free yourself from your past. Write it in accordance to how your mind works to make it truly effective.

If you're an optimist, your pros might be the joy of reuniting with people that have moved away from you due to your problem. Cons might be that you may lose a few friends when you make that change.

If you're more pessimistic, a pro for you might be "you won't have to feel the pain of your friends continuing to shun you or hear your family constantly tell you how terrible of a person you are."

Frame your answers to speak the language your mind most comprehends. In either scenario, if you truly want to change, the pros will outweigh the cons. Why? Because over the past week you have been feeding your mind thoughts of a brighter future. Your mind wants that for you, so it will do whatever it can to assist you in getting there.

For a brief moment, proclaim your reward. Think about moving past your problem; think about how great it will feel to have people seeing you for your heart not your past. Think about the rewards of moving past your problems. This should give you further clarity as we continue to move toward our goal. Keep this in mind. *If more people looked at how their actions affected their future, they'd probably reevaluate some of their actions.*

Some of the greatest doctors, athletes, lawyers, and businessmen never got a chance to be great because the little problems in life clouded the big picture of their life and held them back. They didn't see what they could have been, and as a result, never were. Life got too tough for them, and they didn't think about the rewards of moving past their problems, they drowned in the "now" of the problems.

But that's not you. You have a list of risks and rewards, pros and cons and you will use those in the moments when you feel weak and when you feel like your problems are too much.

Quick Points

- Do you see the glass half full or half empty?
- Do you seek pleasure or avoid pain?
- Right down the risks versus rewards of moving past your problem.
- Use these as motivation when the journey gets tough

Ponder This

Is my mind one that continually seeks pleasure or constantly tries to avoid pain?

How can I use this knowledge to be more effective in my self-talk?

If I continue to do what I'm doing what will happen? What if I do the opposite?

Day 9 – What are you willing to do to fix it?

You often hear of long distance runners who claim they hit "the brick wall" and could no longer continue. Here you either catch your second wind and continue the race or you turn around and go home. Today is that stage. Remember, every problem, no matter how big or small, can't be fixed without the discipline and determination to fix the problem.

A lot of us get to a brick wall in our problems, an impossible barrier, so to speak, and think we can't fix it. Whether it's the fact that we can't turn down another drink, we can't stay faithful to our spouse, or whatever that situation is, usually this is where most people quit. A lot of the times it's because we don't ask ourselves this. What am I willing to do to fix the problem?

That is an infinitely more powerful way to view your situation than to feed your mind with "whelp, this obstacle is too great, I can't get past it." When you think about what you are willing to do to fix it, your mind again comes to your aid. Instead of seeing a brick wall of a problem, you'll find cracks in the wall. Instead of seeing a locked window of opportunity, you'll find that a door may be closed, but it's unlocked.

A willing mind is the most powerful force on earth. This is a difficult and inwardly reflective stage, but it will definitely give you the fuel you need to complete this journey toward a great future. *Don't let the fear of doing what it takes keep you from doing what it takes.* Remember, we set fear aside days ago, so we're moving forward.

As with anything worthwhile, there is always sacrifice. People often think that sacrifice is giving up something to get something, an even trade. That is not sacrifice, it is merely just a barter. A sacrifice should be viewed like an investment. You are giving up something that means a lot to you now in order to gain something in the future that means far much more to you. That is not always a matter of monetary value, but most things in life that truly mean something don't come with a price tag anyways.

In Mark 8:35 tells us that "if you try to keep your life for yourself, you will lose it. But if you are willing to give up your sake for my sake, you will find true life." As Christians we must give up our life to gain a better life in Him. Solving problems is no different. We must give up our "current life," which is linked to our past and our problems, for a better life, the life of our future. A businessman focused on money and work might need to sacrifice some money and hours at the office, for some family time. Keeping the family together will ultimately be worth far more than the money. An alcoholic might need to give up that trip to the bar or that drink.

Again, we understand that this is much more difficult to apply than to read. That is why it's important that you look back at how the problem is affecting you, and then look at your list of rewards for overcoming this problem. We're in this journey because we see the finish line ahead, not because we see the obstacles in front of us.

Doctors and Lawyers spend many years in school, struggling financially, foregoing the fun with their friends, not because they want to be reclusive students, but because they see the end result. They see where these extra years of hard work will place them into a lucrative career, often far superior than that of their peers.

It's also at this stage that you learn if fixing the problem is truly worth it to you. Some of you may look back at your rewards and look ahead at the remainder of the journey and think to yourself, it's not worth it to me. I'm not willing to do what it takes. Sadly, the majority of people get here and do that very thing. That is why the majority of people stuck in their past will remain there.

Good thing is, that is not you. You've committed to the journey, and you will get there. If you are having a hard time thinking about what lengths you are willing to take to fix your problem, go look at your rewards again and see if there might be a stronger reward or benefit for leaving your past. If you already have strong rewards, then you're no doubt brainstorming all of the things you would be willing to do to fix your problem.

We congratulate those that are contemplating ways to fix the problem. Like we said before, every once in a while you have to stand back and pat yourself on the back. You are the one that decided to change and no one knows how far you've come better than you. You've taken great strides, **congratulate yourself.**

Quick Points

- We all hit a "brick wall" at times in our lives.
- Most hit the brick wall and quit, others persevere
- Asking ourselves what we're willing to do to fix a problem is a powerful thought
- If you're struggling to find motivation to think of what you'd do to fix it, reevaluate your rewards

Ponder This

What am I willing to do to tackle my problem and move forward in life?

Do I view sacrifice as a barter or an investment? Explain

Day 10 - Where do you want to be?

Do you see how far you have come since we started this journey almost a week and a half ago? We know we've revisited a lot of tough roads staring back at our past. All of it was necessary in order to truly put a grip on what our past has done to us. We've taken a glimpse into the future but today we're going to stare into it.

In life, it's important to never forget where you came from. Along with that, it's equally important to always know where you're going. Most people, even those that aren't trying to better themselves from their past, don't have a clue as to where they're trying to get to, or what they're trying to do in life.

Do you realize only three percent of people in the world set goals? It should come as no surprise then the top one percent of people own ninety-nine percent of the wealth in the world. We'd be willing to bet they all set goals. This isn't a day to teach you about goal setting. There's plenty of literature on that. What we are doing, however, is focusing on where we want to be.

Any journey or goal can be broken down to a simple three-step process. Figure out where you are, where you want to go, and how to get there. We've found where we are, so let's focus on where we want to go.

We have been building a quiet confidence that you should start to feel by now. It's the confidence that comes with knowing you're on the right path and doing the right thing. That confidence can turn your "want" into a reality. Notice the title of today is where you WANT to be not where you "hope" to be.

Could a runner win a race if there was no finish line? Could a lawyer win a trial if there was never a verdict? We have to have a definitive point we want to reach. We've already decided that we're willing to do whatever it takes to get there. With that mindset, why not set our sights on something great, and not settle for anything less than that.

How would you feel if you were on a plane headed for Los Angeles and the pilot came over the loudspeaker and said, "ladies and gentleman, we're on course for somewhere on the west coast. We haven't decided exactly where but we know we're going to head that way, and hopefully land on a runway somewhere." Would you not run to the cockpit and correct that pilot and make sure he knew to specifically land on the runway in the Los Angeles airport? What if you took a taxi and the driver "thought" he knew where he was taking you, but insisted he'd get you over there in the general vicinity of the area? Would you not want to make sure he knew EXACTLY where he was going?

The key here is specificity. In goal setting people set vague goals like "I want to make more money." If they make one more dollar, congratulations they completed their goal, but is that really what they wanted? The same goes for us. We're going to get through our problems, so we need to think of where we want to be specifically. We may want to be with a loving family, who eats dinner together every night at 6:30 and all talks about their day instead of working late every night. Whatever it is you're trying to get to, that destination in that bright future of yours, make it specific.

Another thing to watch out for is setting a destination that is easy to obtain. Again, don't let fear creep up on you and tell you to limit yourself and what you're capable of. Remember, *you're going through a tough journey, make sure the end is worth it.* You're making sacrifices, and we said that sacrifices are giving up something to get something greater later. Don't settle.

Your future is a blank canvas, and you're sitting here now with all the paintbrushes. The horizon is going to be however you paint it. Wouldn't you rather paint your own future than to just walk along and let someone paint it for you?

If someone gave you a blank check and said "write down any amount you want and it's yours." Would you think to yourself, "Oh, I'll just write down twenty dollars just to be safe?" No, you'd fill that check with so many commas and zeros that it would take twenty years to count all the money. Your destination, where you want to be, is that blank check. It's up to you fill in the "number." You fill in where you want to be.

Don't worry about how we're going to get there, just know that we will. How can we be so sure, you ask? "Don't be anxious about anything, but in every situation, by prayer and petition, with thanksgiving, present your requests to God." – Philippians 4:6

Life is waiting for you sign the check, and tell it what you'd like. Write that check of "where you want to be" in your life. Smile, say thank you, and keep those thoughts in your head. You're going to need them, because tomorrow is a tough climb.

Quick Points

- Never forget where you came from, but always know where you're going
- Decide where you want to be, not where you hope to be
- You have to set specific points of where you'd like to be
- Your future is a blank canvas, it's up to you to paint it

Ponder This

Where do I truly want to be in life?

Are using past experiences a poison or ingredients for a better tomorrow? Explain.

Day 11 – Decision to Change

Get your sharpie, your magic marker, or pen and mark today in your calendar. This will be known as the anniversary of leaving your past behind you, because today is the day you make a decision to change. Consider it a rite of passage as you will, because no matter how you look at it, it's an important day.

Today is the day you decide that you're officially going to make the change. We've weighed the pros and cons, risks and rewards, what you're willing to do to fix, and now we must affirm to ourselves that we must and will change. Don't worry we are not going to jump in the fast lane just yet, we are just proclaiming change.

You might be thinking, "You told us that we must never forget our past," yesterday. And you're right, you shouldn't. With your decision to change today, you no longer look at the past as a bad thing. You view it as a lesson learned in order to help others going forward.

Everything we've done until now was geared toward getting to the mountain, now we'll begin the ascent. This is not a stage to review, but rather to reflect on how far we've come. No different than an athlete who trains for months just to get to the first game, we have walked along a long path just to get to "game day."

Let's glance in the rearview of our lives briefly. The starting point of our journey should seem like a dot on the horizon of your past; yes you have come that far in the past ten days. You may draw on those past experiences in a positive manner, but we will never again visit those places in our realities. Plainly put, you are moving forward. You are at what we call "the point of no return. "

Before we walk through this gate of no return, reflect on your journey thus far. Think about your problem, how it's affected your life, who it has affected, and why you need to change it. Go through your list of rewards, and glance into the future of what you want.

Take your time. What you'll notice is that you are gaining a much clearer picture of both where you were and where you are going. Perhaps you didn't have a picture to begin with, and now you have a defined starting point and a destination point.

Kids in an amusement park always think they want to ride "the big roller coaster." As they get closer, they realize that the roller coaster is bigger than they thought, but they've already come too far. When they get to the roller coaster they often realize it's too late to go back, so they might as well enjoy the ride. They can't turn back now. Even if most amusement parks would let you exit without riding, the roller coaster attendant in your life (you) is going to make you get on it. And when it stops, you won't be on the same side as you were when you entered.

After you take all the time you need to reflect, go ahead and cross this threshold.

You've seen cartoons and movies where the hero of the story must make his way across a shaky rope bridge, thousands of feet in the air, to reach the other side on his heroic quest. Today you are that hero. You must cross that bridge of troubled waters and set your feet firmly on the land of opportunity.

Cross it yet? Good, now story time.

Ancient Greek warriors were masters of motivation and intimidation. Upon landing their warships on opposing soil to battle the enemy, the first command the generals would give is "Burn the Boats." The warriors would then burn the boats, signifying no retreat. It let the opponents know they were there to slaughter the opponents and capture the land, or die in the process.

For the Greeks, there was no turning back. Guess what we're about to do?

You might hesitate, as we're sure some of the Greeks did. But by giving yourself no way out, you must complete your journey. Turn around and look at the bridge you just crossed; now cut the rope. The bridge falls away, there is no turning back. Memory lane is forever just a memory, and no longer an escape route.

Have you ever driven a car forward while looking backward the entire time? Probably not, because you'd almost surely crash. Do you think a sprinter who was focused on looking behind him would beat a runner looking forward? Absolutely not. There's a reason God put your eyes in front of you and not behind you.

This is a journey and we are going to treat it as such. Now that we are truly moving, we will glance in the rearview, but not focus on the rearview. Our focus is what we direct our energies and thoughts toward. Our focus is the culmination of all the steps we've taken, blended together, and directed towards heading in a solid direction.

Think of your problems of the past as various ingredients. Raw eggs, flour, butter, and sugar don't taste that great individually, but mix them together and they make a great "focused" cake.

Reflect on your past experiences, but be sure you're using them as ingredients to create your own focus cake. The beauty of it is that no matter what ingredients life has dealt you, you're free to make your cake as big, glorious, and tasteful as you want. You just have to make the conscious decision to bake the cake.

Quick Points

- Today is a rite of passage, you're making a decision to change
- Glance in the rearview, don't stare at it
- Focus on your future not your past

Ponder This

Am I fully committed to cutting the rope bridge of my past and make the decision to move forward today?

What will removing the negativity from my thoughts allow me to do?

Day 12 – Let it all out

Have you ever been to a yoga class? If you haven't, you probably picture super skinny people in small tights, bending themselves into pretzels and humming like a bee. Yoga has been around for thousands of years, and its methods are effective. If you have ever visited a Bikram Yoga class, you always start with a Pranayama series. This is a breathing exercise that not only helps you control your breath, but also more importantly helps to get rid of all the negativity built up in your body, mind, and soul so that you can focus on the session. This may seem cheesy, but it is the most important part of the class. If you can't let out the negative energy, then your mind will not be able to focus clearly on the class due to having to battle your negative energy while trying to move forward. In a sense, you're continuing to drive forward while looking back.

Yoga might not resonate with you, but I'm sure we've all been so frustrated that we literally want to scream at the top of our lungs, or we hurt so bad we just want to drown our pillows in tears.

We're all human. Therefore we're volatile in our emotions. If we were to move along this journey and not acknowledge that there are times where you feel like you're going to break down, we would be leading you the wrong way. Today is that day where you can break down, and let it all out.

Much like a NASCAR race driver, this is the pit stop of the journey. It's better to get a tune up and get rid of everything negative now in a safe place than to risk having a blowout on the road further down the journey.

This is your final cry, your pre-game mediation, prayer in the morning, loud scream. It can be the punching of the back of your car seat, or running on the treadmill until you can't move. Whatever it is you do to let out all your frustrations (excluding activities that affect others) do them now.

Let go off all the animosity of your past, the hurt, the pain, and the tears. Don't just let it out a little bit, DRAIN IT ALL OUT.

Don't look at crying or hurting as a "weak emotion." View it as release of negativity. Run out that frustration. If you're a boxer, go box until it's gone. If you're a Christian, pray it all out. Take your final exhale, your final silent scream.

This is a great thing. To remove negativity, we open up capacity to fill our lives with more positivity.

Just as one bad apple can spoil a whole bunch, leaving one pent up negative emotion can spoil all of your progress. Simple multiplication can tell you if you have a large positive number multiplied by even the smallest negative number. The result is still negative. IF someone smokes in a "smoking section of the bar" that shares the same air with the "non-smoking section," the result is still smoke filled air. If you had a kiddy pool connected to a large swimming pool, but knew the kids were peeing in their pool, would your water be safe?

In the same manner, harvesting even one negative emotion or feeling can thwart your progress. That one negative emotion is a co-dependent monkey just waiting to jump on your back and cling to you. Let it go now.

Remember the sky is always darkest right before dawn. Today is a stormy day. It may seem dark to you, just remember the sun will be out shortly. Embrace the day for what it is.

"Weeping may endure for a night, but joy comes in the morning." – Psalm 30:5

We are no longer just staring at skeletons in our closet. We are beginning the journey of renewing our hearts. That is why it is vital to get rid of all negative emotion here and today.

Often times a doctor gives you a lot more medicine than you need. He may give you weeks' worth of antibiotics though you feel fine after a day or two. He encourages you to keep taking the medication. Is it because the doctor doesn't believe you'll feel better? No. The doctor knows that remnants of the sickness may be hiding somewhere and if they have a chance, will grow and bring back the sickness all over again. Therefore, the doctor goes overboard to ensure that the sickness is dead and can't build itself back up, so that your body can focus on healing itself – moving forward.

This release today is your antibiotic. You're letting go of all negative energy and emotion until you are either left feeling empty and drained, or filled with nothing but positive energy.

Keep pushing. It's a rough day, but guess what? There's always a silver lining in the dark cloud.

Quick Points

- You have to let out all negative before you can begin to truly build on positive
- When you let it out, let it ALL out.

Ponder This

What negative emotions have you been harboring inside? Did you let them out?

Why is letting it all out a good thing?

Day 13 – The Silver Lining

You have heard the story of the ugly duckling and how that horrendous little duckling transformed into a beautiful swan. You are also probably familiar with ugly little caterpillars spinning themselves into ugly cocoons but ultimately turning into a beautiful butterfly. Are you familiar, however, with how pearls are made?

A pearl doesn't start out as a pearl. It starts out as a piece of sand, bacteria, food particle, or piece of shell. It is an irritant. The clam or oyster goes through a protective process to try and remove the irritant. That process creates a pearl over time.

What is the commonality in all these scenarios? All were outcasts with lowly beginnings and end up being the most desired.

Have you ever flown through a rough storm during the day and got above the clouds? You will notice the sun was shining just as bright as it does on a sunny day. The only difference is we don't see it. Just because you don't see electric currents running in your house doesn't mean electricity isn't there, right?

With our problems and failures, just because we don't see the beauty in them or the lesson in them doesn't mean that they aren't there. That might sound crazy because we've spent all this time admitting to our shortcomings.

Remember we crossed that rope bridge, our past is now just a memory to learn from, steps to build on, but not a path to return to. Yesterday, we let out all of the negativity, the thunderstorms, and rain of our past problems.

Have you ever walked outside after a big storm and looked up to see a sun and a beautiful rainbow? Come outside from yesterday's storm and glance at your past. The negativity is gone. What do you see? If you look hard enough you should see a lesson in the problem and the beauty in the failure.

At this point we need to take back out our book of problems, but this time we're not going to drown in our sorrows. We're going to write down the lessons we've learned from them or the good things that have come out of them.

A mother might have regretted a past spent having a child at an early age. However, that "problem" might have turned into a highly successful child that the mother loves to brag about. A drug dealer may have got caught and went to prison. In prison, he may have had time to slow down and hear the voice of God instead of the fast life of the streets.

No matter what your failure or problem may have been, there is a positive in it somewhere. Finding these positives are the building blocks of a brighter future.

See your problem as a blessing, not a curse. Be thankful that you went through it, and even more thankful that you have the ability to change it. An athlete with an ACL tear might feel like they've hit rock bottom, but when they get through with the rehabilitation process, their "problem knee" ends up being stronger than the normal knee.

God may have been allowing you to go through the problem because He knew that a) not only were you strong enough to handle and preserver through it, but also b) you can be an instrument to help others not repeat the mistake. God says, "You do not realize what I am doing, but later you will understand." – John 13:7. You might already be cracking a smile and seeing ways in which God used you for the greater good, if not, you'll probably see it at the conclusion of this journey.

You will know you're truly starting to see the beauty in your past failures because you will start feeling empowered. You have accepted them, proclaimed change, and are now finding POSITIVE effects of the PROBLEM. Whether you know it or not, even if you don't go another step, you have set the wheels in motion for a better tomorrow.

But we didn't come this far just to admire our progress.

Congratulations! If you have stayed with us whole-heartedly through the past thirteen days then you have done what many are not strong enough to do. Recognizing the skeletons in your closet and owning up to them takes a lot of courage. The courage and humility you have demonstrated has no doubt made you stronger. Emptying out the negative should no doubt have already left you with a better inner-peace with ample room for positivity to come to you.

Bid farewell to that storm of your past. It no longer has any power over you. Dust yourself off, and put a smile on your face, because we're about to enter phase two of the journey.

Quick Points

- Those with lowly beginnings often end up with great endings
- There is beauty in your failures
- Just because you don't see the positives in your failures, doesn't mean they don't exist
- There is always a brighter side to any negative situation

Ponder This

What are the silver linings in the dark clouds of my past?

What are some of the positive attributes of those failures?

Renewal of the Heart

Day 14 – Go to God

When speaking to groups and individuals in our "See my Heart not my Past" series, the most common question we get is "why wasn't this first." *We agree, God should come first in everything.* However, it's at a point in your life when you decide to change, that God is able to more effectively work through you. Today marks that point in our journey where we take action toward moving forward. And yes, it starts with God.

At this point in the journey you may be feeling yourself and thinking you've come a long way. Don't discredit your success, but at the same time don't become conceited with your progress. Inversely, you may still feel lost and not sure of yourself. In either scenario, God can and will straighten out your path if you allow Him too.

If you were to take a trip through an unmarked jungle in the Amazon, would you rather your good friend, who had also never been to the jungle, be your tour guide? Or would you prefer a local native who has navigated the path many times and knows what lies ahead as well as what to watch out for? Pretty easy right?

Would you rather take piano lessons from someone who had never played a piano or Mozart? Would you take business advice from a Fortune 100 CEO or someone who has been unemployed for years? We always trust experts who know the field more than amateurs.

In the path of Life, God is the greatest tour guide. Not only does He know the path, He knows what's ahead, and where trouble lies. He created the path to begin with. We can't tell you that the path will ever be "easy," but we can whole-heartedly tell you that if you cling to God as your tour guide through the rest of this journey, you will arrive at the BEST destination for you, and you will arrive there safely. Want to know what's even better than that? It's Free!

In Proverbs 3:5-6, Solomon tells us to "Trust in the Lord with all your heart and lean not on your own understanding; in all your ways acknowledge Him and He will make your paths straight." The shortest distance between two points is a straight line. God is trying to straighten out our paths. Just as we couldn't navigate through a dense jungle ourselves, we can't stay on a straight path without listening to God.

Have you ever tried to tell a friend or loved one something important during the middle of their favorite show? You can talk until you're blue in the face and it seems like they don't hear you, because they're focused on something else. Does that mean you weren't there talking just because they don't hear you? Many of us feel like "God never talks to me." Do you believe that's true? Or do you think perhaps you haven't gotten close enough to Him to hear Him? Or you haven't stopped focusing on "your TV show" long enough to listen for Him?

Think about a newborn baby for a second. They aren't born and automatically five seconds into the world recognize the unmistakable voices of their Mother and Father. However, over time, as they draw closer to their parents, they start to pick up and hear the voice of their mother and Father. God is no different. The more we cling to Him and listen to Him, the more we will hear His voice. His voice is the one leading us in the direction we know we SHOULD go, even when we take it upon ourselves to take a detour from the safe route.

How would you like it if someone gave you a GPS device that always worked, never got you lost, didn't need batteries, and cost you nothing? That'd be a pretty sweet deal. If you had one and you were in a new city, or new state, would you not get directions from it instead of trying to figure it out yourself? Guess who is your personal GPS? Yep, the Big Guy upstairs. God is constantly trying to keep us on the right path, correct us when we veer from the path, and help us turnaround. Too many of us feel like we know our own way and end up more lost than before.

Your ultimate reason for existence is to please God and do His work. That is comforting for a number of reasons. If you had someone working for you to make you look good, would you not do your best to ensure that they succeeded in making you look good? Wouldn't you supply them with all the resources you could to make their mission a success? Again, God is no different. We are here to serve Him, so rest assured that He will give you the resources to make your journey successful. We just have to ask Him to give us what we need.

Right now, Go to God, and ask Him for the things you know you'll need for the rest of the journey. It may be strength, patience, courage, etc. God isn't going to magically put one million dollars in your bank account if your problem was a financial one. He will open a window of opportunity that allows you to correct the problem and get back on the right path. Since material objects mean nothing to God, He "credits your account" with virtues and things that last. So pray and ask for those and He will give you an unlimited supply.

If that sounds disappointing to you, think about it like this. Does a master painter ask for an already painted canvas? Does a master architect ask for a pre-built house? No, they start off by asking for the tools they need to create a masterpiece. Artists need brushes and easels, architects need supplies. God is supplying you with the virtues you need to create the masterpiece of your life.

There will also be things you will need that you are not aware of yet. Pray that when the time comes, and you face that mountain, that God gives you the tools you need to keep pressing forward.

Finally, pray that above all, He stays with you throughout the remainder of the journey, and speaks louder when you veer from the path.

One of the best ways to make God smile and work for you is to admit that you need Him.

If you're new to prayer, or have never prayed because you don't feel like your prayers can match the immaculate prayers you see on TV, then we're going to let you in on a little secret. There's no hierarchy of prayers that impress God more than another. There is no grade book. If prayers were a school subject for God, they would be a completion grade. You get a hundred if you pray, and a zero if you don't. Every prayer, no matter how lengthy or short, is a perfect prayer.

If you still need help with prayer try this one.

"God, thank you for bringing me this far. I need Help. I need you."

God's GPS will activate and begin working in your life.

Oh yea, that GPS we're speaking of....

God's **P**urpose **S**erved.

Quick Points

- Go to God First.
- God created the path; He can lead you down the safest route.
- You exist to make God look good; He'll give you the tools to succeed in that.
- Ask God for what you need, and ask God to supply you with the things that you don't know you need.
- All prayer is perfect Prayer

Ponder This

What are some virtues that I know I need to ask God for?

What noise in my life keeps me from hearing God? How can I eliminate that?

What will it do if I admit to God that I need His help?

Day 15 – Forgive Yourself

It may seem like we missed a critical step yesterday in our talk with God…the asking for forgiveness for our past transgressions. Don't worry we haven't forgot. You probably have heard this numerous times in your life when people tell you to "lead by example." Forgiveness falls into that phrase. No doubt later in the journey we will want the forgiveness of those that we have hurt. We will also really want God to forgive us of our sins. Many times in life we may have received both of those wishes yet we still feel guilty. Why is that? It's because we haven't forgiven ourselves.

"Forgive us of our sins, just as we forgive those who sin against us…if you forgive those who sin against you, your heavenly Father will forgive you. If you refuse to forgive others, your Father will not forgive your sins." – Matthew 6:12, 14-15.

Yikes. Bet you didn't know there was a contingency clause in that law of the bible in terms of God's forgiveness did you? We have to forgive ourselves so that God can forgive us. A runner on a track relay team can't just start running unless the teammate ahead of him completes his sprint and hands off the baton. God is waiting on you to do your part so that He can take the baton and win the race for you.

You may be thinking, "I humbled myself on day 2 so of course I forgive everybody." Guess what? You're in those "others" that Matthew was talking about. Many of us can't get over the guilt of a past problem therefore we beat ourselves up over it and refuse to forgive ourselves.

At this point you have to remember *there is a fine line between humility and downright beating yourself to the ground.*

Have you ever been to a sporting event and see a team make a huge mistake and hear people say "they shot themselves in the foot tonight?" If you were to attend a boxing match and your favorite boxer came to the ring already bleeding with a swollen eye because he beat himself up in the locker room, do you think he would win? Aside from not being able to win, wouldn't you wonder why on earth he beat himself up for no reason?

When we don't forgive ourselves, that's exactly what we're doing. We're unnecessarily beating ourselves up and decreasing the chances of succeeding. Others will have a hard time forgiving you if the vibe you put off is "don't forgive me, I don't deserve it." By not forgiving yourself, you are in a sense, continuing to put your hand on a hot stove. Yes, we have had mistakes and problems, and yes there may have been some skeletons in the closet, but you should know that the skeletons are trying hard to become a productive part of your future. They don't want to sit there as a dirty bag of bones in your closet.

By not forgiving yourself, you're glorifying your past, not helping it. If you're watching television and the person in the room with you gasps and yells don't look, what's the first thing you do? You look. Not forgiving yourself works in that same reverse manner. It's going to get you the opposite result of its intended purpose.

It's essential that we learn to forgive ourselves because not doing so can affect our future emotional stability. We may have cut the rope bridge and moved on from our past physically, but remember our mind and our problem walk hand in hand. If we continue to withhold forgiveness from ourselves, we are only holding on to the past we're trying to move on from.

If someone tossed you a live grenade, chances are you wouldn't sit there and look at it and think about what it's going to do. No you'd get it as far away from you as you could as quickly as you could. By not forgiving yourself, you are holding an emotional grenade of self-hate that could explode at any time.

By forgiving yourself, you are not "letting yourself off the hook." You are not saying, okay everything's perfect. You're just giving yourself a chance to continue to grow and progress. Forgiving others is hard. Forgiving yourself is infinitely harder. Remind yourself that self-forgiveness is another way of saying, "I don't hate myself." In fact take it further. Look in the mirror and tell yourself "I love myself." We have to begin to see the change in ourselves and that begins with being happy and believing in ourselves so that we can continue to improve.

By forgiving yourself, you are stripping away the power your past problems have over you. You are taking the gas out of your past's engine, the wind out of its sails. Not to mention forgiving yourself is a lot like lifting weights. The actual process breaks you down a bit, but it literally makes you stronger as you heal from it.

This is just a minor setback to prepare for a major comeback.

It is a tough step. Be specific in what you're forgiving yourself for. Don't just say, "Okay self, you're forgiven." Forgive yourself for detailed things. By doing so, you are removing any power that past mistake had over you and strengthening yourself as you continue to make progress in the journey.

After you forgive yourself, ask God to forgive you. You'll instantly feel like the weight of the world has been lifted off your shoulders when you God's forgiveness and have forgiven yourself. This phase of the journey is an instrumental step in renewing our hearts. When we forgive ourselves we can further use our past mistakes as a fuel to a brighter future.

Remember, our past problems are beneficial when they remind us of God's forgiveness. When we remember that, we remember that He loves us and He will help us to see better days.

We're on the right path.... let's move along...

Quick Points

- You have to forgive yourself before God or others can forgive you.
- There is a difference in humility and beating yourself down
- Withholding forgiveness is holding onto our past
- This is a minor setback to prepare for a major comeback

Ponder This

What do I need to specifically forgive myself for?

What emotional grenades am I holding onto? How can I let them go?

Day 16 – Visualize Succeeding

You often see elite athletes make game-winning heroic plays to win championships for their teams in the final seconds. In their post-game interviews, they shrug it off and say they've hit that shot a thousand times in their mind, while we sit and marvel at their courage in the clutch situation.

The fact of the matter is this. These athletes have played this play over in their mind thousands of times to the point it becomes natural. They visualize themselves making that play.

If you've lived in your house long enough then you know how to get around it and find where you put things, because every day you visually see the house. Similarly, whatever career you have, you can probably do the repetitive tasks easily because you've done them over and over.

Here's a secret. Your mind cannot tell the difference between you actually doing something and doing it mentally in your head.

Fact. Several studies have been conducted on Olympic sprinters hooked to biofeedback equipment. Half were told to run a real race, the other half were told to run the race in their minds. Guess what the result was? Identical. That being said, it's apparent that visualization is a key to aiding people in their success.

It's always easier to do something once you've done it. Have you ever traveled somewhere across town for the first time and it seems like it takes forever? However, the more you frequent the same spot, the shorter the drive seems. It's because you've been there, and it's no longer new.

When you visualize succeeding, or overcoming your problems, you're giving yourself a chance to walk through the steps without actually walking through them. This can save you a lot of time and heartache if you take it seriously. Do you think a public speaker would deliver a better speech if they got up there and just winged it or if they had prepared a speech and practiced it dozens of times? The same goes for your journey. The more you practice what lies ahead in your mind, visualizing all the actions in a successful journey, the better prepared you are going to be when the adversities head your way. Why, because you've already "hit that shot," "or defeated that adversity" a thousand times. The real one is no different.

How many times have you watched your favorite action flick or love-story movie (ladies) and thought to yourself, "I wish I was that person." We'd all like to be movie stars. Visualizing your success allows you to not only be the movie star, you can also write the script and direct the film, how cool is that?

Days ago we visualized being where we want to be, the final destination. The old adage says, "If you don't enjoy the journey, you won't enjoy the prize." You wouldn't want to go see a brand new movie you've been dying to see and fast forward to the final scene would you? You want to see the entire movie, the highs, the lows, and the triumph right? You must do the same with your life.

You have to visualize overcoming your problem, battling adversities, climbing that road to a successful future. The focus now is on the actions involved in climbing toward your destination that we set a few days back.

You should make a habit of doing this daily, even if it's for just 3-5 minutes. Sit in a quiet place where you know you won't be distracted.

Turn off your cell phones and other things that can clutter your mind or interrupt your thoughts.

Close your eyes and picture yourself sitting in the room you're in. Now get up in your mind, and walk out the door into the world.

Picture yourself confident and happy taking the steps you feel are necessary to get to where you want to go in life. Picture your friends and family and those you've hurt all smiling and supportive of the new you as you continue to improve.

Do you want to know if the visualization exercise worked? Ask yourself this. Do you feel better? You should. If you watch the movie of yourself becoming the person you want to be you can't help but feel good. Remember your mind doesn't know if the action was real or imagined. That is why scary dreams often mess up our entire next day and have us feeling anxious. That is why we get giddy at the thought of going on a date with that person we've been courting for a while. In our minds it is always real.

That is another reason we need to make sure our visualization of where we are headed is all positive. The mind tricks is a double-edged sword, because if negativity finds a way to creep back in, your mind will believe that too. It will believe that "there's no way you can do it," or that the road is impossible. Stay positive and visualize vivid pictures. The more details you put into your visualizations, the more your mind will think it is real. The more your mind believes it, the easier the situation will be when you really do face it.

Fans of Star Wars always envy the Jedi's because of the Jedi Mind Tricks they play on others to get their way. You are that Jedi. The Force is in you. Jedi Mind Trick your way into a brighter future and it will happen.

Proverbs 23:7 Solomon states, "As a Man thinks, he is." See yourself moving toward your future, and watch how much more quickly it happens.

Quick Points

- Your mind can't tell the difference between visualizing doing something and actually doing it
- The more vivid your visualization is, the more real it will seem to your mind
- As a Man thinks, He Is

Ponder This

How do you visualize yourself overcoming your problem?

What vivid details do you see that make you excited about the journey?

Day 17 – Devise a Plan

The greatest generals in war don't walk around enemy territories aimlessly just hoping a battle doesn't happen. On the Contraire, they not only expect the enemy to be there, they think about every tactic the enemy could try to use to be able to defeat them. Simply put, they are prepared. It's no secret we can't avoid, run, or hide from our problems or the things that trigger our problems. If we do run, it only increases fear and allows the problem to grow.

We recently spoke with a man who used to have an addiction to marijuana. He explained to us that he removed himself from it, and went on to become a successful businessman, never being around marijuana. Almost twenty years later he went to a concert with his daughter and smelled marijuana in the crowd. Instantly he was brought back to craving weed. That's not to say that removing yourself from a trigger or a problem is a bad thing, it is however, more beneficial to prepare to face and defeat whatever is holding you back.

You are in the battle of your life. You are the general, leading your life's troops against the enemy we identified as a problem. In any competition, whether it is sports, war, or business, the opposition always attacks what they know your weakness to be. Your problem and your past knows your weakness, and it knows your trigger. Guess where it will attack you? It's almost funny isn't it? When we think about it out loud it seems so silly that our past continues to trip us up the same way over and over.

In war, its kill or be killed. One of two things happens. You let your past, your surroundings or negative peers pull your trigger on you, or you initiate your own trigger.... only this time it's a trigger that will send you into your future, not your past.

Expanding on what we did in day 8, we're Marty McFly sitting in our Delorean again, setting the year we are about to go forward to, also known as devising the plan to get toward our future.

Would a blind person or someone with 20/20 vision have a better chance of driving a car safely from one side of the country to the other? Do you know anyone who would purposely put on a blindfold and try and drive? Why is it then that we do so with our own lives? *If you don't plan for your future, you are living blindly.* Your opposition, (pronounced problem), has planned very well. It has planned not only to stop your progress, it has planned to make you go backwards and lose yourself in your past. Your only hope of beating it is to plan.

Sun Tzu said, "Strategy without tactics is the slowest route to victory. Tactics without strategy is the noise before defeat." Taking action is good, but taking action without any sort of plan is no different than swimming around in circles in the middle of the ocean, thinking you're getting close to land. All you're doing is causing a commotion to let the predators know where you are.

I'm sure you know someone who is an extremely "hard-worker." Yet over the years they never make any progress in life even though they work hard. Ask that person where they are trying to get to or what they are trying to accomplish. You'll be surprised to find most don't know. If you don't know where you're headed, any road will take you there.

Great boxers become great, not solely because of their offensive skills, but because of all the time spent studying their opponents. After studying, they know what the opponent will do, how they will move, and are able to think of ways to counter the opponent's attacks. Study yourself first, realize where your weaknesses are. That's where your problem and your past will attack you. Find ways to turn your weaknesses into strengths.

In a hive there is one queen bee, and numerous worker bees. The bees know the queen bee's survival is paramount for the survival of their species. They stop at nothing to protect her so that she may reproduce. Your trigger is that queen bee. Your thoughts and planning should be aimed at protecting someone else from pulling your trigger. When someone else pulls your trigger, it still affects you. This can be emotional, mental, or spiritual suicide.

Your planning is vital. You will, beyond a shadow of a doubt, be tested. Biblically this is true. "And you shall remember all the way which the Lord your God has led you in the wilderness these forty years, that he might humble you, testing you, to know what was in your, whether you would keep his commands or not." - Deuteronomy 8-2. You said a few days ago that you were ready to change and proclaimed change. You went to God because you were serious about change, He wants to believe you and He will help you to succeed. However, He will test you to make sure you really want it. The devil is looking to make sure you don't progress, so you will be tested on all sides.

Devise your plan. You already know where your problems will attack you. Make plans to strengthen those past weaknesses. It may come straight at you or disguised as a harmless situation or friend, beware. Remember those past weaknesses no longer define you, you control them. You pull your own triggers, not the other way around. Just as in grade school, the more tests you pass and progress, the harder the tests become, but there is always a reward at the end.

Quick Points

- Great generals plan for victory
- You let others pull your triggers or you learn to control and pull your own
- Know how the past problem will attack you so you can counter it

Ponder This

What is my plan to get toward my future destination?

In what ways will my past try and attack me? What are my weaknesses?

Day 18 – Replace the Bad with a Good Alternative

Have you ever noticed that every building and every airplane have an emergency escape route? The routes are designed to get you to safety in the event that an emergency situation arises. During emergencies there is a lot of commotion and panic due to the impending harm from the emergency. The escape routes get you to a calm safe. There are fires in your life, and you need an escape route for those emergencies. Escape routes in our lives are merely finding a good alternative to a seemingly bad situation. Just as apartment buildings have escape routes, so should you.

Yesterday we devised a plan. Devising your escape route should be no different. If you don't plan for how to handle the emergencies, known as the sudden unexpected reemergence of your past problem, you can't escape it safely. If there was no planned fire escape in a building, you may run from one fire into a bigger one. That's why there is planning to make sure the escape route helps you truly escape.

If a fire was in your room, you wouldn't sit there and ignore it, would you? If you heard smoke alarms or felt the heat in the next room, you wouldn't casually stroll into that room would you? Why is it then that often we ignore our problems and think they'll go away, or we casually stroll into worse problems?

The key here is to have a POSITIVE escape route. A positive escape route for an alcoholic who is tempted to go to the bar is not to go get a twelve pack of beer or a bottle of vodka, and drink at the house. A positive out for someone tempted to cheat is not to go home and watch a pornographic movie instead and think, "Well at least I didn't cheat."

A positive alternative instead might be talking to a friend who is willing to listen and give you positive advice about why you're feeling how you are. (Not a friend who says "let's go to the bar and talk about it.") A positive escape might be a hobby you had as a kid before life's problems became what they are. It might be a hobby that you got too busy to continue, but doing so may bring you joy.

There is no right or wrong or good or bad, just make sure your good alternative pushes you closer toward the future you desire not the past you're trying to avoid.

To someone who has a problem stemming from being overly introverted, a positive might be to go out and socialize. That same positive for the introvert could be a negative for someone whose problem stems from being out all the time and the lifestyle that can be associated with it.

Only you truly know if your escape route is a good one for you. Here is a little trick to help you realize if it is a good escape or not. Ask yourself the following question. Do I have to find a way to justify why my escape is a positive one? If you have to justify to yourself or others why it is a good escape, chances are your pride has snuck up and put blinders on you again.

If you're in a building right now, look at the fire escape. You will notice there are always numerous escape plans. Why, because there is a chance that the certain escape you want to use is blocked off. The gym may be closed, you might not have the book you read, or your go-to friend may be unavailable. Be sure and map out a couple of escape options.

Look at an elevator next time you're near one. They all say the same thing. In case of a fire, use the stairs. That means you may have a more difficult time working to get to safety than taking the easy "automatic ride." Having an escape route may take work. It's not easy to "avoid the fire" so to speak. You may have to do everything in your power to avoid being burned by your past. However, just as you would rather climb 50 flights of stairs than to burn in a fire, it is beneficial to your life to stop at nothing to escape the fires in your life.

Once again, we are not permanently running from our past. We will put out the fire, but when it sneaks up on us we must first get to safety before we begin to battle the fire.

A question we often get asked is "what if I don't have an escape?" The answer is that you always do. There is always that escape door that is open and never blocked, His name is God. No fire, whether it's the burning of your past, or hell's flames, can keep God from being there to help you escape. In Matthew 11:28-30, Jesus says "Come to Me, all who are weary and heavy-laden, and I will give you rest." Take my yoke upon you, and learn from me, for I am gentle and humble in heart; and you shall find rest for your souls. "For My yoke is easy, and my load is light."

Sometimes that may be the only escape you have open, but it is definitely and always the best one. Unlike other escapes, He will give you the energy and heart to continue the escape when you are tired from climbing all those stairs.

Become that flight attendant in your own life. Let yourself know where your escape routes are "in the event of an emergency." That way when a problem hits, you are able to take that negative and turn it into a positive.

Wouldn't you like to be able to replace the bills in your life (negative) with checks (positive)? Your future wants the same for you. It is banking on you replacing those negative old habits with positive alternatives.

Quick Points

- All buildings and planes have escape routes.
- Escape routes in your life help you replace negatives with positives
- Escape routes should not lead you into a bigger problem

Ponder This

What are my escape routes in life?

Where do my escape routes lead me to?

What people can help me design my escape routes?

Day 19 – Broadcast your Change

Muhammad Ali was arguably one of the most outspoken greatest boxers to ever live. He was notorious for predicting which round he would finish off his opponent. These were not small predictions amongst a group of friends. These were national news conferences with diagrams and poems. He unapologetically let the world know constantly that "He was the Greatest of All Time." His actions backed that. Ali would nearly always defeat his opponent in his prediction, if not sooner. If he were predicting these rounds and getting knocked out, would he have any credibility? Not at all. But due to his outspoken predictions coupled with his consistent ability to show he was good to his word, there were no doubt a lot of anxious boxing fans during the rounds Ali predicted the knockout.

We all want to be great at something. Today you have the opportunity to become the Muhammad Ali of your problem, and you're going to win by knockout in whichever round you decide. Are we going to be vocal in our change? Yes. You may not come up with press conferences and little raps to announce your change, but we will unapologetically tell ourselves and those around us that we have defeated our problem, and it is no longer a formidable opponent for us.

When you proclaim something out loud, your mind has a strange way of putting its wheels in motion to make it happen. If you want your dog to sit, stay, or do a trick, but never tell it out loud what to do, how will it do what it's supposed to? If you want your kids to do something, don't you have to tell them to do it? Your mind works similarly. It is waiting on you to proclaim victory and to announce that you have defeated your past, even before you do.

This is not getting out a bullhorn and walking down the street saying, "I am the greatest." However, you will be unafraid to tell people you have changed. What happens when you proclaim something or make a prediction? People watch to see if it comes through. People bet either for or against you.

Seems easy right? Talk is cheap right? The phrase talk is cheap should have an asterisk next to it. At the bottom of the page the asterisk should say, "Talk is cheap, unless coupled with action." Ali's words were far from cheap, but it's because he backed it consistently with actions. Words alone equal wind. Words backed with action are known by another name – Momentum. When you demonstrate and start living what you're talking about, your words become powerful. They mean something. It's almost an added accountability you put on yourself when you broadcast your change to others.

If you were running in a big race like the Olympics wouldn't you want people to know, especially those you care about? If you won the race wouldn't you for sure want to broadcast it? You are in the race with your past to get to your future and therefore should let the world know. Now if you haven't trained properly for the race, you might not tell people for fear you will lose. If you felt you were the best and knew you trained the best, would you not predict the win?

We always marvel at those people who decide they are going to lose a bunch of weight, tell everyone they are dieting, and lose tons of weight. What's the number one question someone who was fat and ends up getting chiseled up abs and a great body is asked? "How did you do it?" That person now becomes an influence to others who have the same problems but we're afraid to admit it to people or didn't know how to change it.

We have to tell you another secret. The problem that you're dealing with where you feel like "no one would understand," is shared by thousands if not more around the world. You're not the first to go through it, you're not the only one dealing with it, nor will you be the last. You can't help others that went through it, but by broadcasting your change and rising above the problem, you become an example and a leader to others who battle what you do. Do you see it? You're already becoming Muhammad Ali.

We must stress to you, **action is important.** When you broadcast change, everyone watches. That is why you hear the term "practice what you preach." People that weren't even interested before, now care. Those that care about you definitely will pay attention. They may not believe you at this point, but deep down they hope it is true.

You have trained, and you are ready. We've had a long journey thus far. It was preparation for this press conference of your life. It was all preparing you for today where you announce to the world that you are superior to your problem and your past. Cockiness is when you say something outlandish that you can't back up. Confidence is saying something that you truly believe in, even if it hasn't happened yet. We want to be confident when we announce our change. Speaking the truth is not conceit.

"Be diligent to present yourself approved to God, a worker who does not need to be ashamed, rightly dividing the word of truth" – 2 Timothy 2:15. God told his people not to be ashamed of the truth. Your change is honest, it's true, and your heart is renewed, so there is no reason to keep quiet about this marvelous win. Let the world know how far you've come, how far you're going, and more importantly what God has helped you overcome.

Tell your problem, "I am the greatest." Now get ready. The bell is about to ring and the fight is about to start.

Quick Points

- Voice your change
- Words without action, are just words
- Words with action become momentum and strength
- Conceit is when you just talk. Confidence is when you mean what you talk about

Ponder This

What will I say in my press conference to the world announcing my change?

What actions will I take to give meaning to my words?

Day 20 – Ask for Forgiveness

The opening bell has rung and the real fight starts now. Your strength, faith, perseverance, and especially your humility will be tested today. We have forgiven ourselves and ask God for forgiveness. We have come to grips with our past and decided to make a change. Today, we start the process of creating a better future by taking steps to heal relationships with loved ones stemming from the wounds are past has left.

Have you ever wanted something really bad, and knew the person you were around could give it to you, yet they don't? Later on after the opportunity passes, you kick yourself and ask yourself "why didn't I just ask?" Forgiveness requires you to ask for it before it can be granted.

Ancient Chinese philosopher Lao Tzu said, "A journey of a thousand miles starts with the first step." You don't get to your destination in one step, but the first step is important. First, realize that asking for forgiveness isn't going to automatically fix a long history of hurt. It is not a cure-all. It is however, a monumental first step in showing your loved ones that you have humbled yourself and you are genuinely working to restore those relationships.

Asking for forgiveness shows others that you understand your actions hurt them, that you take full responsibility for your past and problems, and you are taking strides to change your future and heal those wounds. Strangely, while we're asking others for forgiveness, you are still helping yourself. Asking allows you to defeat your past by giving you peace of mind knowing you are taking genuine action to right your wrongs.

By asking for forgiveness you are taking real strides forward, not just retracing your steps. When asking for forgiveness, don't look for sympathy. You're not after sympathy, you're after change and healing relationships. Selfish people are concerned about themselves, you are concerned about the other person's thoughts and feelings.

Have you ever given someone a heartfelt gift, and sat there in anticipation of what they'll say as they open it? They open the gift but say nothing. Deep down all you want is to hear a simple "thank you" and it will mean the world to you. Asking for forgiveness is saying thank you, in a sense, for someone not completely abandoning you despite your flaws and problems.

We always want an answer when we ask a question. We won't hear the answer unless we listen. We've apologized for the ways we know that we've hurt the person. However, often times we hurt people in ways we didn't realize, or they're affected by different things than we thought they would be.

Swallow a humility pill. Ok ready?

The second part of asking for forgiveness is asking the person you care about to tell you how they've been hurt by what you've done. Really listen and take note of what they're saying. Often this, more than the asking for forgiveness, will mean more to those you are asking. It shows them that you want to hear from them how they've been hurt by your actions. We've learned earlier in our journey that it's impossible to fix a problem when you don't know what it is. It is impossible to fix a relationship when you're not fully aware of the animosity or hurt the other person has.

There will be times when you want to rebut what they say, or explain your side of the story…. do neither. Sit there, listen, and pay attention. This isn't easy to do, but will be a monumental step in creating your better future.

The people you ask may get upset when telling you how much they were hurt, but this is a natural part of the healing process. However, we don't want to leave them with mental pictures of all the times you've hurt them through your problem.

The final step in asking forgiveness for others is by asking what you can do to fix it. Brace yourself to hear all kinds of answers. Remember in day nine we said we'd be willing to do anything to fix our problem. These people you seek forgiveness from are no doubt in the happy picture of your future, therefore, you have to let them know you're willing to do what it takes to restore what you've broken down. Let them know you're not looking for an instant reconciliation based on your word alone. You can ask them to open their heart and mind enough to allow you to demonstrate through your actions that you are the change you are proclaiming. This will give people at a greater sense of ease instead of merely thinking this is another ploy from the book of lies or problems.

Remember there is a reason that the people that care about you are still in your life. They want you to change. They are on your team even if they are guarded. Deep down they have hearts willing to forgive. It may take time for those walls to come down. Remember, you agreed it's worth it, but be patient. Show change. When they see you've forgiven yourself, God has forgiven you, and you're willing to do what it takes to fix your relationship, they'll eventually come around.

Forgiveness is healing, plainly put. It's true healing, not just putting Band-Aids on a big problem. James states, "Therefore confess your sins to each other and pray for each other so that you may be healed. The prayer of a righteous man is powerful and effective." – James 5:16

Not everyone is going to jump on your bandwagon immediately. Be patient. Pray with those people and for those people and ask that they pray for you. Just like the verse says, the prayer of a RIGHTEOUS man is powerful. It can shatter those guarded walls built up by what you were in your past.

Congratulations, you took a big step today.

Quick Points

- To get forgiveness, you have to ask for it
- Forgiveness is the first step in mending relationships, not the only step
- We must ask how our problem affected the other person and what we can do to fix it.
- Forgiveness takes time. Be patient

Ponder This

Who Have I hurt?

In what ways have I hurt them? (Write down what they say)

What can I do to fix it? (Ask them)

Day 21 – Accountability

Accountability is a word that makes immature people groan. They look at accountability as added unnecessary responsibility, additional blameworthiness, or extra liability. They say this because they know accountability puts extra eyes on you. Deep down they despise accountability, because they know they will let everyone down. They aren't ready for change.

That is immature, non-growing people, not you. As part of your progress, you welcome accountability. Accountability, to you, is the mile-marker sign on the road that let you know you're going the right way. It's the GPS that helps keep you on the direct path to your destination.

Earlier we said that it's better to do things for others to live a full-life than to do everything for yourself. The same can be said of accountability. It is great to motivate yourself and hold yourself accountable for your actions, but it is infinitely more powerful when you have others to help keep you accountable. Remember, we're trying to build relationships that we've damaged. Accountability is the glue that helps hold those relationships together until they further develop.

In the Oscar movie awards there is always awards for best supporting actor and actress. They award this in the film industry because they recognize the importance of a great supporting cast to make a great movie. Two days ago we broadcasted our change. Think of accountability as the support system to make that a reality. It's your life, you're the star, and you write the script, however, no one has ever had a great movie with themselves as the only one in it.

Along those lines, it's important that you pick a great supporting cast. Supporting cast doesn't mean "back-ups," It literally means the cast of people around you that support you. If someone doesn't want you to succeed, they're not going to support you. That being said, you can't ask for accountability from people who have no interest in your progress. Those that care about your future are going to be more inclined to keep you on that road to a brighter future.

Too many people get their support system from what we call "yes men." Yes men are those people around you that agree with everything you do or say. We want positive people in your life, but there is a big difference in support and agreeing. Some of the best support you can have is people you ask to keep you accountable and watch you like a hawk.

Have you ever had a demanding boss, coach, or teacher that watches your every move? You may dislike them, but you are well aware of what you're doing if you know they're watching, are you not? Sometimes those pessimistic people are great at keeping you in line. Yes men, on the other hand, are cancers to your success. They give you a false sense of progress, when really you are making none. If you're trying to walk to your favorite restaurant a mile away, could you get there on a treadmill? You'd just be spinning your wheels. "Yes men" are treadmills. You may feel like you're making progress but you're really not getting anywhere.

In professional sports, instant replay has become an increasingly important part of the game. Pro sports move at a fast pace, and referees make mistakes. The more cameras that capture the play, the better the play can be analyzed and the correct call can be made. Your life moves at a fast pace. You are the referee. Sometimes in the midst of the actions you may make a mistake and not realize it. An accountability partner is good, but even they may miss your mistakes sometimes. That is why it is good to have more eyes on you, more accountability partners. These are not people that are looking for you to do wrong. They are looking to make sure they give you an accurate description of what you are doing. You know where you are going. They are there to help make sure you stay on that road.

Accountability partners are the air-traffic controllers in our life that help us land at the final destination that we originally set out for. "The way of the fool is right in his own eyes, but a wise man listens to counsel." – Proverbs 12:15.

Successful businesses are those that remain accountable to the metrics they have set. Great athletic teams are successful in large part because of the accountability everyone on the team has in doing their job. A large part of the success in your life will come from the company you choose and their devotion to keeping you accountable.

It's your movie. Pick a great supporting cast.

Quick Points

- Accountability is a support system
- There is a big difference in genuine support and "yes men"
- Find as many genuine accountability partners as you can. The more eyes that are on you, the more conscious effort you will make to stay on the right path.

Ponder This

Who will give me honest feedback and direction?

What's the difference in support and agreeing?

Day 22 – Speak Out against Former Ways

In sporting events we always love it when a star player plays a game against their former team. In business we like to see an employee go to a rival organization. "Tell-all" books fly off the shelves as people reveal the darkest secrets of something they used to be a part of. There is a certain level of intrigue whenever someone's allegiance changes. None of those are as talked about and followed as when someone voluntarily speaks out against their former ways. The speech is more powerful. If someone used to do something and are now saying the other way is better, people want to know why. They listen.

That is why alcohol rehab programs often have guest speakers that were former alcoholics. Former gang leaders are impactful in their speeches to youth when speaking out on the dangers of gang activity. Former drug dealers are highly effective in speaking against selling drugs. A lot of this stems from people thinking that if someone lived a life in one way, and completely transformed, there must be a reason that they changed.

There was once a man who would go city to city dragging people out of churches, making up false stories, and having them killed. He took pride in having good Christians put to death, and devoted his life to doing so. This man, Paul, changed his ways and end up being one of the greatest tools for Christianity with all his published scriptures in the New Testament of the bible.

Have you ever noticed how small little words from someone speaking out against an issue can snowball into a large scandal? In 2001, a reporter spoke out against corporate giant Enron, via an article. That led to the uncovering of one of the largest corporate scandals in history and caused a multi-billion dollar company to go bankrupt.

Speech can be a powerful tool, especially when the speech is aimed at those with whom the speaker used to side with.

If you were car shopping would you rather buy a car from a dealer that said "well um, I think that possibly this car might do some of things that you want a car to do," or would you buy from a dealer that told you "This car not only does what you want, it is also packed with many more features that you will love?" You'd probably go with the more confident speaker. If you were seeking investment advice, would you go with a stockbroker that said "well I hope this makes you money and not lose too much," or the broker that says "this is a sure bet, you can't lose with this stock?" Again, you'd go with the more confident broker.

Confidence is key to believability. Speak out against the past and problems you used to have. This, aside from showing others you are serious about your change, helps separate you from your past and helps you side with your future. The bibles said Paul would go into temples and speak BOLDLY for Christ. He was highly successful in turning people to Christianity. Would he have been as successful if he would have gone into the temples and said "I used to be against Christianity but now I kind of got a good feeling that maybe this following God thing might work?" He may have converted a couple of people but would not have been nearly as successful in converting the masses.

When you're speaking out against the problems you used to have, you're not just speaking to the people you're trying to heal relationships with. It is important to speak to those who are still caught in those same problems. They are the ones who really need to hear what you're saying. Remember, this journey isn't just a solo journey. It is a journey of leadership as well.

You will face opposition in this. You will be called a sell-out, a hypocrite, and a traitor. Don't listen. That talk is coming from those who don't have the courage to change like you. They are the people that got to day one of the journey and quit. A hypocrite is not someone who changes sides. A hypocrite is someone who speaks against one thing, but knowingly continues to do that very same thing with no thought to even change. They are conmen. That is not you. You're speaking against your problem, but you are no longer living the life of that problem. You may face it and be tempted to relapse, but your heart is set on change.

Weak-minded people often belittle those who change. It is not because of the change, but because it's easier to try and keep someone down and discredit them, than it is to have the courage to make the journey toward a bright future. You know how hard the journey is, after all, you're in it. Don't hold it against those people, if anything, it should give you more motivation to succeed. Those that share your problems may need to see someone they know change before they begin to. Not everyone was meant to build the road. Some people only want to follow it.

Faith is believing without seeing. However, most people need to believe to see. Be that change that they need to see, so that they can follow your path.

Speak boldly. Let your actions be bolder.

Quick Points

- Confidence is key when speaking out against your past ways
- Those speaking out against a life they used to live can be a highly effective tool in helping others
- Hypocrisy is not speaking against a former way of life, it's speaking against it while continuing to live it, with no thought of changing

Ponder This

Who are some people that share my problems that I should speak to?

Who is ridiculing my change?

Why am I meant to be a leader and not a follower?

Day 23 – Become the Help

If someone you loved was coming to visit you for the first time, would you give them directions that took them through dangerous neighborhoods, bad roads, or would you give them safe directions? Have you ever gone in to a store and found an amazing sale on a product you have been wanting? Don't you want to tell others about the great savings? When we know a better way of doing something based on our experience, we tell those around us so they can reap the benefits of our knowledge.

Earlier in our journey we learned to see our past as a lesson not as a failure. We ourselves have grown from our mistakes. Today it's time to help others. Experience can be the greatest teacher. If you know a road leads to a dead end, wouldn't you tell someone heading down that road to turn around? Sometimes people miss signs on the road. The road of life doesn't have signs posted by the highway department. You must be the caution sign to others. You have to be the one to warn people of detours, wrong-ways, and potholes. Sometimes you have to be the flashing red lights telling people to STOP. How would you like to drive by a wreck knowing you could have prevented it had you told someone about the upcoming road hazards? Chances are you'd feel terrible. Having been down the road ourselves, it is our duty to prevent others from wrecking their lives or having blowouts. Essentially we are keeping people off paths of destruction and turning them towards roads of success.

Abraham Lincoln once said, "If I turn an enemy into a friend, have I not defeated the enemy?" This can be said of your former problems or way of life. By using the experiences of your past, you can become a teacher that helps many people. If you help people avoid your mistakes, they no longer look at you as a person with a problem. They look at you as a helping teacher.

It takes far less energy to keep someone from falling down than to pick somebody up. Helping people that have fallen can take a toll on us emotionally, physically, mentally, and spiritually. While that's important to do, it's far better to prevent the fall in the first place. You don't have to rescue people if you help prevent the danger in the first place. Often times our problems are bigger than us, therefore, we rely on God. God put you through the problems you have endured because He knew you were strong enough to handle it and be the shoulders to carry others who don't share your strength. Don't believe us? You've come this far, that is proof enough of your strength.

Automakers thoroughly test cars before they enter the market. They have test dummies that go through the impacts of the wrecks and collisions to see how different wrecks and situations will affect the masses when the car reaches the market. What if the test dummy didn't report accurate results to the computers about the severity of the injuries sustained in wrecks? There would be a high likelihood that many people would be severely injured or worse. In life, we are those crash dummies. We have been through the collisions of our past and thrown around by our problems. If we don't "report the results of the collision" to others, then they too will have to go through it. However, if we openly speak about the dangers of the path and the wrecks it will cause in life, we can save lives. We are the seatbelts that save lives. We are the crossing guards that guide people to the correct road.

Now that you've grown in your journey, you should no doubt see the world with more clarity. When our problems lose power over us, we have more clarity. Look around you. Somewhere, probably closer to you than you think, someone is struggling with the same problems that you used to have. Be there for that person. Remember, you don't have to complete the journey to lead others. You need only to be ahead of them. You may be the only warning signs they ever have.

When you speak about your experiences to help others, you won't be looked at as the person you once were. Someone who does the same negative thing over and over is known as a fool while someone who speaks about the negative things they used to do is known as wise. When you grow from your past you are viewed as having knowledge. You definitely won't lack in credibility because you lived it. You know firsthand the ins and outs of the problems you faced.

You have indeed turned those skeletons that used to take up closet space into noble assistants for you in your journey.

Quick Points

- By using your experiences, you can become a teacher to others.
- It takes less energy to prevent a fall than to pick someone up
- To be a leader you don't have to have finished the journey; you just have to be a step ahead of the people you're teaching
- Repeating mistakes over and over makes you a fool; Speaking on experience makes you wise.

Ponder This

Who around me can I help save from going down the
path I went down?

Is it easier to prevent or repair? Why?

Day 24 – Reinforcement of Mission

Time heals wounds but time can also bring contentment and complacency. Complacency causes us to lose track of our original mission. Businesses that have dominated their industry for decades often get complacent. Competitors who were focused on becoming the best often pass the complacent business. When you've had a long journey like we've had thus far, it's often times easy to lose focus due to the adversity in the journey. We may feel guilt creeping up on us, or we may not have had as receptive of a forgiveness session with others as we had hoped. No matter the reason, today is a day to regroup and refocus.

If things are going well and you're moving along through this journey, it is still good to take a day to refresh and make sure you're still on the road you wanted to head down. Our cell phones work fine yet we still charge them to keep them working. Every few months we get maintenance and oil changes in our vehicles, not because they're broken, but we just do it to refresh the vehicle maintained so that it will have increased longevity.

Reinforcement is nothing more than looking back at the reasons we decided to change in the first place. Whether it's for your children, visions of your future, or wherever you're trying to get to in life, the most important thing is that you once again visualize your final destination.

Picture your life as a garden and reinforcement as the watering of the garden. The water's job is to keep the plants fresh and to aid in their growth. Have you ever been outside in hot temperatures and a cool breeze floats by? Have you ever received an unplanned bonus at your job? They are refreshing, are they not?

We've been climbing this mountain of our destiny for over three weeks. It's very easy to break down in a strenuous journey if you don't rest. We are stretching and renewing our minds today, however this is as close to a "day off" as you will get on the journey.

Doctors ask that we get annual physicals not because something is wrong but to ensure that everything is right. If you're on the right track, this is preventative maintenance. In the event that something is wrong, that allows you to catch it before it becomes a big problem.

Reinforcing to yourself why you are on this path is preventative maintenance. We are double checking our map, our path, and making sure that we are still headed toward the destination that we set out with on day one.

The larger a contractor wants a building to be, the more he must reinforce it with solid metals and concrete. The contractor knows that without solid reinforcing beams, the building will eventually crumble. Along those same lines, you need to make sure that you reinforce your goals with strong mental pictures of where you are trying to go. If a contractor tried to reinforce a 100-story building with straw and grass, the building would fall. If you put weak images in your mind that don't really drive you to want to succeed more, you are setting yourself up to crumble before we reach the end of our journey.

On day ten we set the destination point of our future into our GPS. Let's revisit that day to make sure we still care about that destination. There is a chance, due to your growth that you realize you are capable of an even better future and you may adjust your route accordingly today. Do not, by any means, settle for less than you originally set out for. *You should always allow yourself to push further, but never to come up shorter.*

Don't just casually picture your future. Visualize it in detail. It's no doubt that today's high-end high definition televisions give us an infinite clearer picture than the old black and white televisions. We marvel at the detail because it makes the picture look real. Again, today is no different. The more vivid images you put into your mind, the more your mind will want to succeed. We are renewing our hearts and with proper thoughts of your future, your heart should start beating faster. You should be anxious to start tomorrow.

Throughout the bible, God reinforces several of His principles by repeating them in scriptures. He sends us constant reminders as a way of reminding us the importance of following his instruction. This is why He encourages us to pray, read scripture, and listen for Him. He does that so that He can remind us of the rewards in heaven that await us if we stay on the right path. Scripture and prayer are the spiritual food that refreshes us daily. Positive reinforcement of your original goal will help to ensure that you stay fresh.

This second leg of the journey was tough, and you should again congratulate yourself. We have fought the skeletons in our closets, and we have turned our past into assistants for our future. We have renewed our hearts. We're getting close to the summit of our journey, but remember it's called a home stretch. That doesn't mean we're there yet. The peak, however, is in sight. It's time for the final leg of our journey.

Rest up. Tomorrow we begin to bypass our past.

Quick Points

- Time can cause complacency
- You must rest and reflect at times to keep your mind and body fresh
- Paint vivid pictures of where you're heading in your mind. This positive reinforcement will give you the energy you need to persevere in the last part of our journey
- God reinforces his principles to remind of us our rewards; do the same in your life

Ponder This

What details can I add to the picture of my bright future that will make it more meaningful than it was when I first thought about it?

Am I capable of going further than my original goal?

If so, what changes do I need to make to adjust my GPS?

Bypass the Past

Day 25 – Backlash of Change

Mahatma Gandhi once said, "First they ignore you, then they laugh at you, then they fight you, then you win." You're probably nodding in agreement because you are starting to feel it, the backlash of change. Earlier when we proclaimed change, many around you probably ignored you thinking it was all talk. They no doubt watched you and in their minds probably laughed at you as you continued to read this book and go through the steps. A strange thing happens when people realize you renew your heart, all of the sudden people see it. Those around you that want you to grow are starting to become filled with hope.

However, there are those around you that do not share the same love of your change. Often our associates and friends are those that are like-minded and indulge in the same problems and lifestyles as us. It's no secret that this journey is difficult and you've been courageous in the steps you've taken to see a brighter future. Remember it's easier for others to try and pull you down than to try and lift themselves up, which is why there is so much negativity in the world.

Remember, when they say you're the same as you used to be or that this is temporary, it's NOT PERSONAL. When they try and knock you, or when you face the backlash of change, they're not speaking to you. When those around you speak negatively of your change it's simply them trying to justify in their minds that they are not lazy. No one wants to admit they could have worked hard and made the change too if they started where you did, yet they remained there while you grew. In a sense they are trying to blow out your candles so that their candle appears brighter.

It's also tough when you face backlash from those around you that you didn't expect it from. No doubt, there were people that always told you that you need to change. However, now that you've demonstrated a noticeable change, those same people are singing a different tune. Again, it's not personal. They might not have your same problems, but their pride knows they have problems too and have done nothing to fix it, unlike yourself.

Have you ever sprayed bug or ant spray into a hornet's nest or an ant bed? Do the ants or bees just sit there calmly and die? No, they sprint out of hiding as quickly as they can. They scramble because they know the pesticide is an effective tool that will become the end of them. Hate, Jealousy, and Envy are those bees and hornets. Your positive mindset and your change is the ant killer. The more you're around those who harbor hatred and jealousy, the more your positive is going to bring out the negative in them.

Again, don't take it personally. Look at the jealousy and envy as giving a last ditch effort to try and knock you down. Only they can't, because we've built a solid foundation and we're set on finishing this journey.

People will also speak out against you because of their own insecurities. Everyone has dreams and ambitions, and some know they will never do what it takes to reach them. They see you, on the other hand, close to your future and they start feeling like your success will cast a shadow on their lives. Their insecurities come out and they speak down on you. Again, don't take it personally. Take it as a compliment to people recognizing your change.

Remember, this is your journey. Those people saying your change isn't genuine weren't there with you when you were battling those skeletons in your closet alone. They weren't there as you swallowed your pride, humbled yourself, and spent time praying and planning. How then, could they tell you about your own journey? Don't let their insecurities discredit your walk.

By now, you should be so focused on the peak of your destination that you aren't even worried about others" thoughts and opinions if they are merely those that try and push you back down the road you've come from. Remember weeks ago we cut the rope bridge to our past, so to fall back would be to fall off the cliff, and that's not us. We are moving forward.

Jesus, who never did one wrong thing, was hated, cussed at, spat upon, beaten and killed because of his continuation of his path toward Heaven and his positive heart and spirit. If He had to deal with that, you shouldn't expect that the same wouldn't happen to you. (Don't worry, we don't believe you'll be beaten and killed.) However, you will face opposition. That is part of the journey.

Just remind yourself that their insults and belittling of you and your journey is really admiration that their pride won't allow them to divulge. What someone who is not trying to help you thinks about you has absolutely nothing to do with you. That is their opinion.

There are plenty of armchair quarterbacks who sit in the stands of collegiate and professional sports talking about which plays the coaches and teams should have executed. They weren't spending the countless hours the coach spent that week in preparation for the game in deciding what plays should be ran. That is why they are in the stands and not in the game. You're on the playing field focused on winning the game; don't listen to the fans in the nickel bleachers.

Keep pushing. People are watching now more than ever. The same people who knock you now, will come to you for advice in changing their lives. As Gandhi said, "then you win." Helping them will be another victory in your journey.

Quick Points

- Don't take insults personally
- With change always comes opposition
- Stay focused on the end of the journey and you won't be affected by what others negative thoughts are

Ponder This

What are some things people are saying about me and how can I remind myself that it's not personal?

Why is backlash a good thing?

Day 26 – Smile to prevent the Cry

Yesterday hurt did it not? You may be thinking, "are you guys emotionless?" You're correct. The truth many times is hard to deal with." We understand that we're all human and have emotions. None of us are impervious to hurtful words that others hurl at us, especially those that we care about. That is why we stress the positive mindset in this last leg of our journey.

Have you ever gotten salt in your eyes, or pepper spray, or any disabling chemical that makes it hard to see? When your eyes water and blur, the last thing you are thinking about is progress in life, your thoughts change to restoring your vision not moving forward in life.

Tears in this part of our journey only blur our vision of where we're going. No doubt the words were hurtful and sting, but we must keep moving. We said earlier that God's goodness outweighs the schemes of the Devil. Therefore, *good outweighs bad.* Not that all tears are bad tears, but a genuine smile will outweigh sorrowful tears any day. Smiles are more powerful than you might think.

Very quickly, look in the mirror and smile at yourself for a full minute. Try it. You will notice it's impossible to be in a bad mood when you are smiling. You may laugh at yourself for doing what you deem a silly exercise, but it does help you feel better. It has an even bigger effect on those that see it. When a stranger smiles at you is your first thought, "I can't believe that idiot was smiling at me, what were they thinking?!" No, you would probably smile back. When we smile around others, it lets others around us know that we are happy. Those that support us will be filled with more hope because they know the smiles are a sign of continued momentum. Those that did not support us are now paying even more attention to you because the smile shows them that their negative words aren't bothering you.

For a second let's pretend that you are going on two job interviews in rival companies right next door to each other. In the first business, you walk into a hostile environment with screaming going on, employees moping around, everyone looking depressed, and no one looks like they want to be there. You walk into the second interview and are greeted by a smiling receptionist, employees high-fiving each other on a big sale, and a boss who is planning a reward party for his employee's hard work. Without knowing anything about either company, which would you choose? *The second one.* That is because everyone wants to be associated with a good thing. Positive interactions are magnetic and draw people towards them.

Have you ever heard loud music and a lot of people from a party next door to you? It makes you wonder what is going on. You may not know your neighbor but you are intrigued by the good time they seem to be having.

When we smile, despite our inner pain, it draws people towards us. It makes people want to know the secret to our happiness. You're on a path to a great future. Most people are satisfied just trying to find some sort of happiness in their lives. Despite your trials, you're smiling. Therefore, as before, you are now the wise man in the area of happiness. You are obviously walking that path.

It is vital that you remember that your ability to smile isn't just for you. It is for those around you. Even those that are jealous of you, deep down want to change. They are watching you intently to see so that they may believe. They may need to see the smile on your face more than you need to give one. Do it for them.

The darkest hour is right before the sunrise. We no doubt have been facing dark hours with the backlash we've been receiving. After rain comes, the sun always dries it up. In that manner, happiness dries up sadness, even if it's artificial happiness by way of a forced smile.

If you can learn to smile when times are tough, then imagine how joyous you are going to be in the good times. This journey has been an emotional roller coaster, but we are too close to the summit of our journey's end to feel low again.

Many expert mountain climbers that attempt to climb Mt. Everest, the largest mountain in the world, freeze to death in the final stages of reaching the summit because they stop. They start feeling the cold, and seeing excuses as to why they can't finish. When they don't progress, they freeze to death.

We are too close now to stop and worry. We can't stop and look back behind us and become struck with fear over how far we've climbed. We can't let those tears overwhelm us. We must smile and look ahead. We are almost there.

Quick Points

- It's important to maintain a positive mindset in the last stages of our journey
- When events cloud your vision, you lose focus on your intended target
- Smiles aren't just for you; others need to see them as well
- Happiness outweighs sadness, so put happiness into the world around you

Ponder This

What are some things I can think of to keep a smile on my face even though I may be hurting inside?

What will my smile do for myself and others?

Day 27 – Consistency / Persistence

When you were a baby do you think your parents said your name one time and you automatically knew it from then on? Do you think great athletes become great overnight? The answer to all of these questions is absolutely not. All of the above mentioned were created through consistency.

If you really think about a river that flows down a mountain through a valley, you would be surprised at how it was formed. Most think that rivers were just created in the sides of mountains and have been there since the beginning of time. The truth is that rain falls down the mountain, and over the course of thousands of years or more, the trail that rain drops fall down the mountain slowly and methodically turns into the rivers that they are today.

Most everyone has tried some sort of diet at some point in their lifetime. There are no natural ways of losing a lot of weight instantly. Regardless of what the latest and greatest fads and diet pills tell you, the only way to healthily lose weight is through a consistent diet regime. The point is that consistency is the path by which all things improve to be their best.

Nothing can grow without proper nourishment. The more you feed something, whether it is a person, lifestyle, or habit, the faster it will grow.

Even your bad habits or old problems were formed through consistent adherence to feeding those problems. Today we are making a conscious effort to reinforce positive consistent habits. We are feeding solutions not problems.

Just as we drew upon the experiences of our past to become teachers for others, it's equally important to remember the positive steps and strides you've taken in the past near-month. Repeating these steps, affirmations, and methods to grow will ultimately make them become second nature to you.

A few days ago we talked about reinforcement of our destinations in our mind. Consistency is applying the steps we've taken continually until it becomes part of subconscious. Nothing becomes second nature overnight.

When something becomes second nature to us, we no longer have to think about it. Our mind and body go into "auto-pilot" and do it for us. Again, our minds are going to make habits out of whatever we feed it. We replaced the bad with the good alternatives earlier. Let's focus on engraining those escape routes into our minds so that they become second nature.

Your body has no limit on the processes it can automate without your knowledge. When you boot up a computer, there are certain programs that the computer automatically knows to bring up. Your mind works like that when you wake up and thankfully so.
What would happen if your mind forgot how to tell your body to breathe correctly? What if you had to teach yourself how to walk or how to talk every single morning when you wake up? We don't think about that or the millions of other things our body does for us, but it does so. It does most things because of the consistency and repetition of doing a certain action.

Most of us have a morning routine that we seem to do in our sleep. We may hit the snooze button twice, wake up, drag ourselves to the bathroom and brush our teeth, or head to the kitchen and make coffee. We don't think about it, we just do it. It is just routine to us. How did it become routine? It became that way through repetition and consistency in doing the same thing repeatedly.

More than anything it's important that we keep a positive mindset and a drive to reach our bright future running over and over in our mind. If you are consistent in nothing else, at least be consistent in taking at least one step towards your future daily, no matter how big or small it is.

Marathon runners don't wake up one day and say, "I can run 26.2 miles today." They build up to that distance over a series of consistent workouts. If a runner said, I'll work out today, but then took a few days off, and repeated the process, wouldn't it take them a lot longer to get to their goal of being able to run 26 miles?

Consistency not only creates good habits, it allows us to reach our goals faster. The truth is, there are days on this journey, and there will always be days, where you just don't feel like doing something. You may not want to go to work every day, but you consistently go because you know you need to. When we build consistent mindsets, that consistency will continue to carry us toward our futures even on days we don't feel like it. After all, it's what you do when you don't feel like it that determines your level of success.

As is the case with everything beneficial, you may not like it when you're doing it, but you'll always be glad you did. Focus on taking consistent steps in your journey toward a great future. The best way to walk a long journey is one step at a time.

Take those consistent steps, as we get closer to our goal. The future we want is no longer just on the horizon, it's almost within our grasp. Let's keep moving forward.

Quick points

- Consistency turns rain drops into great rivers
- Habits come from consistent thoughts and actions you feed your mind (good or bad)
- When you're consistent, it becomes second-nature, and your mind does it for you
- Consistency helps us to reach our goals quicker than if we were sporadic in our approach

Ponder This

What thoughts and actions do I need to be consciously aware of in order to make consistent strides toward where I want to be in life?

Are my thoughts feeding my solutions or my problems? How?

Day 28 – Facing Yourself

Olympic one hundred meter sprinters train for years to prepare for one ten second showdown. In every Heroic story the hero must ultimately face his Nemesis. You can grow and move along your journey, but eventually you have to face the problem that started this journey in the first place.

We have spent the last month studying our problems, renewing our hearts, and walking down the road together. Beyond extreme adversity lies great success. Simply put, adversity is the doorstep to success.

We have made great strides in defeating our problem, but today we must deal with our past problem directly. This is the big fight we've been preparing for. This is the steep climb towards the top of the mountain.

Have you ever had a big presentation at your school or office or taken a test that you knew you weren't prepared for? Aren't you stressed when you go to it because you could have been more prepared? In that same test or presentation, have you seen others that are prepared walk in with a smile on their face, anxious to begin? The difference is in *the preparation*. The good news is you are prepared. Along this journey we have stressed the importance of going through the steps correctly, even if it takes more time. We did this so that you would be fully prepared for today.

Have you ever wondered why steroids are unsafe for people? They make you big and strong. However while they make your muscles, on the outside, grow quickly, the rest of your body including tendons and ligaments don't grow as fast. The result is that your body is not fully prepared to handle the muscle gain and it often leads to injury. In the same way, if you had skipped steps or not been devoted to completing each step, you would not be ready for today. You could tell yourself you were ready, similar to a mental steroid, but deep down you know you weren't ready.

Remember this is our life, and our past is behind us, so in order to find it, we have to look in our rearview. It's time to face the mirror.

In a boxing match, it is said that you win or lose the fight before the fight ever starts. Sun Tzu said, "The general who is victorious makes many calculations in the temple before the war is fought. The general who loses makes few calculations." Most of us have butterflies in our stomachs before a big event. You can enter this battle calm knowing you were prepared.

So how do we face our past? Very easily, for the most part we already have, now we must put it all together. The victory is in our minds and our hearts. Let's revisit the problem we used to have. Look at how it used to hurt us, and look at the path it had our lives headed down. Look back at the day you decided to fix the problem, make changes and the day you cut the rope bridge, leaving your past back on the other side.

What you will notice is the hurt and worry you had when you were going through those times originally have not been replaced by a sense of peace. The past that used to look like a monster in front of you has now been reduced to a stepping stone to help you continue moving forward. The past has tried its best to hold on to you by throwing fear toward you. Guilt, friends and families have said you will never change. But you have changed; therefore those attacks don't rattle or break you.

Most importantly, the knockout punch you've delivered your past is that you no longer spend your life walking backwards; you don't regress toward your past.

Have you ever been in a relationship that's not good for you and finally realize it? What do you do to move on? You walk away from that bad relationship and move toward your new one.

The best way to get over something is to move away from it. By leaving your past behind and sprinting toward your future, you're sending a message to your past that you will no longer be associated with it, because you're in a new relationship – with your future.

Accepting and being at ease with the mistakes you made is the surest way to victory. Your past may have won numerous battles; it may have beaten you down throughout the fight. Have you ever watched a Rocky movie? There comes a point in every main fight where Rocky encourages the opponent to hit him. He starts to enjoy it. That is the turning point because Rocky no longer lets the opponent's hits affect him. At that point, he then begins to go on the offensive. You are Rocky. Your past's punches no longer feel strong as it tries to stop you. The more you laugh at the inferiority of your past, the stronger you will feel.

Seeing you smile and laugh at its attempts to bring you down, your past, much like a tired opponent in the late rounds of a fight, will lose faith in its ability to win. You are killing the will of your problem's ability to defeat you.

Congratulations, you have just beaten the biggest opponent in your life. You have defeated your nemesis. You have defeated the darker side of yourself!

Quick Points

- We often train years for one important battle
- Preparation is the key to success
- The best way to get over something is to move past it

Ponder This

What was my past's last ditch efforts to try and defeat me?

How will I make sure that the problem doesn't win?

Day 29 – Shut Out Your Past

There is no looking back. We left our past lying in the ring as we celebrated our victory. We will not be granting our past a rematch, because we are moving forward in our careers. We are shutting the door. Yesterday we bid farewell to our past, and it was the last time we'd be seeing it. Today we are grabbing that shovel and burying that past.

At Halloween people often dress up in costumes and disguises. It's almost as if they are a new person, hard to recognize. Have you ever seen someone that you haven't seen in years and you don't realize it's them because of how much they have changed? Over the course of this journey you have changed. You are not the person you were when you were victim to your problems in day one.

Your past, though it may seek ways to always find you, won't recognize the new you. That's because you are not the person it was used to bullying. If it can't find you, then the only way to cross your past again is for you to go to it. We are burying the past and there will be no revisiting it.

Much like an athlete that has rehabilitated a broken bone and come back stronger than ever, you have rehabbed yourself, and the problem is no longer a problem. The past hurt you a lot, but you have healed yourself. The past is now nothing but a story or a notch on your belt of experience. You don't get offended when others ask you about it now because you know that they ask because you are a teacher, not because they want to hold you to who you were. People that meet you now would have no idea that you used to be that way.

Have you met people like that? Whether it is great husbands who you find out were once ladies' men, or strong women who you find out had a very promiscuous past, we often don't believe it because who they are doesn't reflect who they were. Those people have moved on from their past and now reveal their heart. That is YOU.

Speaking about it is only because you are preventing others from going down that path, or helping bring them out of it. The past itself doesn't affect you.

When a cold breeze comes through your house, you close the doors and windows. This effectively shuts out the cold. In sports when you shut out an opponent it means that the other team did not even score a single point against you. Today you are shutting out your past. It can't score against you. It has been defeated. You are leaving it out in the cold while you enjoy the warmth of your renewed heart and future all around you. When the sun shines bright, it's hot outside. We call it a bright future because it is filled with warmth and happiness.

What would happen if we would have left that door slightly cracked or if we stopped playing at the end of the game and allowed the opponent a chance to score? Or what if a boxer left the door open for a potential rematch with the opponent he defeated? The problem would have a small chance of coming back to defeat us. That is why it is imperative that we shut the door and lock it, not allowing our past to be a part of our future in any way.

"Shut out all of your past except that which will help you with your tomorrows" – Sir William Osler. You have defeated your past so you can pick and choose the lessons and things you want to take from it. Take what is good, and leave what is not.

If someone were to let you walk into your favorite clothing store and get as much apparel as you want for free, would you go in the back and dig through the trash for items or would you get the newest trends and fashions in the store? You would take the best stuff. Your past had some good lessons and it has a trash bin. You are allowed to pick the great lessons from it that help you move forward and discard the trash. Leave it there.

When we get through a big problem or catch a break in life, we often say "Thank God." You have beaten the problem, so thank God. He has been there for you when no one else was. It is because of Him and only Him that you were able to move from who you were to who you are.

"Therefore, if anyone is in Christ, he is a new creation; old things have passed away, behold; all things have become new." – 2 Corinthians 5:17.

You have renewed your heart. You have become a new person. You are a person capable of creating a future not being swallowed by a past. The past has passed away, your skeletons have been buried and you have become the new you. Be the new you and let people begin to **see your heart not your past.**

Quick Points

- There is no looking back; shut the door on your past
- Your past can't find you because it won't even recognize the new you
- When you shut the door on your old problems, shut it completely
- Because of God you were able to become the new you, Thank Him

Ponder This

What steps can I take to make sure I lock the door and shut out my past?

How can I show God I'm thankful for the victory?

Day 30 – See My Heart Not My Past

You have just crossed the finish line of this race. You have reached the peak of the mountain, and you have reached the destination you set out to reach. You have reached a new YOU. You are now the person in your future that you set out to be. It's time for people to *see your heart not your past.*

A lot of times in life we don't give people a chance because of their past. A lot of time it's because they still demonstrate characteristics of their past. We all have things we're not proud of but the only way to change a past is to do better in the future. Over this journey you have done that. It is important that you continue the new you even though this journey is over.

In order for you to do that, you must remember that you are not who you were. Therefore you cannot act how you used to. The new you is poised, positive, and your mindset is moving forward.

More importantly, there are many people just now getting to the starting line of where you were. In the same way you didn't want to be judged when you were changing, you must extend that same courtesy to others. They say it's always easier on the other side. Serve as a mentor for those trying to change. The best way to show your heart is to demonstrate that you have one. Take your focus off their past and help them to see that a bright future is possible for them to reach.

The heart of a person is a reflection of who a person is, not their past. We take special care of babies because they have not fully developed yet, and they are fragile. At the start of our journey we took baby steps, and now we have taken great strides and won the race. We had to crawl before we could walk; walk before we could run, run before we could climb, and climb before we could reach the mountain peak.

Tell others to see your heart not your past. The way for them to see your heart is through your actions. Put good in the world. Make it your mission to be an example to others through your words and your actions. Expand upon the steps you took. Remember we made sure that our word backs our actions, therefore becoming stronger. When you are consistent in that, your words will hold a lot of merit.

Tank drivers in armies aren't worried about people shooting bullets at the tank, because the tank is bullet proof. It has a hard exterior that enemy weapons can't penetrate. It enables the tank to move forward confidently.

You have become impenetrable to your past and anyone that tries to bring it into your future. Anyone worth your while won't be trying to knock you down. Those that try and knock you down aren't worth your time. People hoping to bring negativity back in your life are the people that need help the most. Those are the people that need you, not the other way around. Remember their shots aren't personal, it stems from pride and their inability to express that they desire to walk the path you did, regardless of what they say.

Do we stop now? No. You have changed and are showing your heart not your past. Showing your heart is a continual process. There is always a chance to grow, always a chance to make your future brighter.

It is people who are blind to growth that say "once bad, always bad." Everyone that you look up to at some point took the journey you just completed in his or her own way. Just as you looked up to them, people will look up to you, because you are genuine.

People will judge you for the new you. Make your heart impenetrable to regressing. Display a positive and giving heart.

Remember when you see a heart, you see the truth.

- See my Heart not my Past

Quick Points

- You have reached the peak, you have completed the journey
- Others are trying to follow your path, be a mentor to them
- For people to see your heart you must show that you have one
- When you see a heart, you see the truth

Ponder This

How will I continue to grow from here?

What is the best way to show the world my heart?

Epilogue

You have reached your destination, but remember this...

The finish line is the starting line of an overachiever.

Discussion Questions

Chapter 1

Do I want to continue to let my past dictate my future or will I admit I have a problem so that I can begin fixing it?

Who is at fault for everything? Why is this a good thing?

Why does masking a problem make the situation worse?

What should I do when I realize I am headed the wrong way?

Chapter 2

In what ways do I most struggle with pride?

What does foolish pride do?

Why do I hold onto pride when I know it weighs me down?

Chapter 3

What has fear kept you from doing?

What happens when you ignore problems in your life?

Chapter 4

What is the difference between an issue and a problem?

What are my issues?

What is my problem?

Chapter 5

How are my problems affecting my quality of life?

What areas of my life are my problems having residual negative effects on?

Am I fixing problems or putting Band-Aids on issues?

Chapter 6

Who has my problem affected and how deeply can I see that it has affected them?

In what ways did my problem grow to be this big?

Chapter 7

What are the triggers in your life?

What is the button sequence to initiate your triggers?

Chapter 8

Is my mind one that continually seeks pleasure or constantly tries to avoid pain?

 How can I use this knowledge to be more effective in my self-talk?

If I continue to do what I am doing what will happen? What if I do the opposite?

Chapter 9

What am I willing to do to tackle my problem and move forward in life?

Do I view sacrifice as a barter or an investment? Explain

Chapter 10

Where do I truly want to be in life?

Are you using past experiences as a poison or ingredients for a better tomorrow? Explain.

Chapter 11

Am I fully committed to cutting the rope bridge of my past and make the decision to move forward today?

What will removing the negativity from my thoughts allow me to do?

Chapter 12

What negative emotions have you been harboring inside? Did you let them out?

Why is letting it all out a good thing?

Chapter 13

What are the silver linings in the dark clouds of my past?

What are some of the positive attributes of those failures?

Chapter 14

What are some virtues that I know I need to ask God for?

What noise in my life keeps me from hearing God? How can I eliminate that?

What will it do if I admit to God that I need His help?

Chapter 15

What do I need to specifically forgive myself for?

What emotional grenades am I holding onto? How can I let them go?

Chapter 16

How do you visualize yourself overcoming your problem?

What vivid details do you see that make you excited about the journey?

Chapter 17

What is my plan to get toward my future destination?

In what ways will my past try and attack me? What are my weaknesses?

Chapter 18

What are my escape routes in life?

Where do my escape routes lead me to?

What people can help me design my escape routes?

Chapter 19

What will I say in my press conference to the world announcing my change?

What actions will I take to give meaning to my words?

Chapter 20

Who have I hurt?

In what ways have I hurt them? (Write down what they say)

What can I do to fix it? (Ask them)

Chapter 21

Who will give me honest feedback and direction?

What is the difference in support and agreeing?

Chapter 22

Who are some people that share my problems that I should speak to?

Who is ridiculing my change?

Why am I meant to be a leader and not a follower?

Chapter 23

Who around me can I help save from going down the path I went down?

Is it easier to prevent or repair? Why?

Chapter 24

What details can I add to the picture of my bright future that will make it more meaningful than it was when I first thought about it?

Am I capable of going further than my original goal?

If so, what changes do I need to make to adjust my GPS?

Chapter 25

What are some things people are saying about me and how can I remind myself that it is not personal?

Why is backlash a good thing?

Chapter 26

What are some things I can think of to keep a smile on my face even though I may be hurting inside?

What will my smile do for myself and others?

Chapter 27

What thoughts and actions do I need to be consciously aware of in order to make consistent strides toward where I want to be in life?

Are my thoughts feeding my solutions or my problems? How?

Chapter 28

What was my past's last ditch efforts to try and defeat me?

How will I make sure that the problem does not win?

Chapter 29

What steps can I take to make sure I lock the door and shut out my past?

How can I show God I am thankful for the victory?

Chapter 30

How will I continue to grow from here?

What is the best way to show the world my heart?

About Rehab Time

Rehab Time **(Renew Every Heart and Body)** is the bridge between the secular and the sacred. By erasing the dividing line that separates the two, we are able to bring people from all walks of life together for a common cause which is to uplift positivity, educate, and empower people in their everyday life.

Our mission is to serve as a worldwide community that instinctively promotes change for the better by uplifting, empowering and demonstrating that "change starts with you," from the inside out, through the development of faith, self, fitness, relationships and leadership.

Our vision is to become the worldwide resource community for people to become wholesome individuals.

We at Rehab Time know that through our change, we create the future, and we hold ourselves accountable for demonstrating the change in which we wish to see in our online and physical communities.

To find out more about the Rehab Time Organizations visit us at **http://www.RehabTime.org** or **http://www.TeamRehabTime.com**

Visit Trent Shelton at **http://www.TrentShelton.com**
Visit Baylor Barbee at **http://www.BaylorBarbee.com**